Making
Room

Making Room

Living with One Another in Our True Humanity

Linda A. Rex

WESTBOW
PRESS®
A DIVISION OF THOMAS NELSON
& ZONDERVAN

Copyright © 2018 Linda A. Rex.

All rights reserved. No part of this book may be used or reproduced by any means, graphic, electronic, or mechanical, including photocopying, recording, taping or by any information storage retrieval system without the written permission of the author except in the case of brief quotations embodied in critical articles and reviews.

WestBow Press books may be ordered through booksellers or by contacting:

WestBow Press
A Division of Thomas Nelson & Zondervan
1663 Liberty Drive
Bloomington, IN 47403
www.westbowpress.com
1 (866) 928-1240

Because of the dynamic nature of the Internet, any web addresses or links contained in this book may have changed since publication and may no longer be valid. The views expressed in this work are solely those of the author and do not necessarily reflect the views of the publisher, and the publisher hereby disclaims any responsibility for them.

Any people depicted in stock imagery provided by Getty Images are models, and such images are being used for illustrative purposes only.
Certain stock imagery © Getty Images.

Scripture quotations taken from the New American Standard Bible® (NASB), Copyright © 1960, 1962, 1963, 1968, 1971, 1972, 1973, 1975, 1977, 1995 by The Lockman Foundation Used by permission. www.Lockman.org

This book is a work of non-fiction. Unless otherwise noted, the author and the publisher make no explicit guarantees as to the accuracy of the information contained in this book and in some cases, names of people and places have been altered to protect their privacy.

ISBN: 978-1-9736-3312-9 (sc)
ISBN: 978-1-9736-3311-2 (hc)
ISBN: 978-1-9736-3313-6 (e)

Library of Congress Control Number: 2018907717

Print information available on the last page.

WestBow Press rev. date: 7/5/2018

Isn't the fundamental problem at the root of all others we are facing in our world today how to make room for each and every person to be counted as an equal, to be validated for his or her own unique personhood, and to live with every other person in a harmony and unity in which each is respectful of self, others, and the environment in which she or he lives?

Contents

Acknowledgments ix
Preface xi
Overwhelm Me xv

Chapter 1	Sharing the Same Earth	1
Chapter 2	Making Room	5
Chapter 3	It's Just Not Who We Are	9
Chapter 4	My Next of Kin	13
Chapter 5	A Chance Meeting with My Sister	17
Chapter 6	Our Unifying Distinctions	21
Chapter 7	The "Righteous" Life	25
Chapter 8	Being Human—Who Am I?	29
Chapter 9	The Whole Message	32
Chapter 10	The Curses and the Ten Commandments	36
Chapter 11	The Divine Aggressor	40
Chapter 12	The Battle against Despair	43
Chapter 13	Something from Nothing	47
Chapter 14	Stop Hiding and Start Finding	50
Chapter 15	Putting New Wine in This Old Wineskin	53
Chapter 16	Rain in the Desert	56
Chapter 17	What Does It Mean to Repent and Believe?	59
Chapter 18	Learning to Lament	63
Chapter 19	Leaving It All for Love	70
Chapter 20	It's Tempting, But …	73
Chapter 21	"Is it Love or Is It Magic?"	77

Chapter 22	Is Grace Really Enough?	80
Chapter 23	Growing in Knowing	83
Chapter 24	Loving the Unseen and Invisible	86
Chapter 25	Leaving behind the Ignorance of Prejudice	89
Chapter 26	Intercellular Living	92
Chapter 27	Heart-Sharing	97
Chapter 28	God up Close	100
Chapter 29	Face to Face	104
Chapter 30	Covenant Relationships and Our God of Grace	108
Chapter 31	Breathing God's Air	112

You Blew My Mind 115
About the Author 117

Acknowledgments

Many thanks to all my brothers and sisters in Christ who have prayed for me and offered me feedback as I put this project together. Thank you, Brad and Paula Plumlee, for your unwavering support and encouragement. Thank you, Dr. John McKenna and Dr. Gary Deddo, for your affirmation, and Ted Johnston, for your encouragement to keep writing. Thanks to all of you for your grace and love expressed to me in so many ways.

Preface

Sometimes it's embarrassing to be a human being. After all, we've been around for thousands of years, and we're still doing the same stupid stuff. We're still killing each other, abusing one another—you name it—we still do it, even when we know it is hurtful and destructive.

I have to admit I'm no different from anyone else. I can't condemn the person who is a murderer because I know, for all intents and purposes, I have murdered people in my own thoughts and words. There really isn't any difference between the two; the first is just more obvious and out there, and the consequences are more direct and exacting than those that come with angry, evil thoughts and motives.

The past couple decades in the news, we have seen more stories about terrorism and the efforts of certain groups of people to impose their beliefs upon innocent, well-meaning people through violence and fear. We've seen the videos and heard the stories about people who have been injured and killed and their lives ruined by these terrorists. Some of us have personally experienced these evils. We can experience fear and anxiety in our everyday lives because of what these terrorists have done and are doing.

In America, we are experiencing a renewed concern with regard to the ongoing divisions between people of different races and ethnicities. We may have thought these issues were dealt with, but in truth, they linger on because we as humans haven't left behind our prejudices and the grudges we hold against one another. We continue to act and speak in ways that perpetuate these divisions.

Recently, I started to watch a video where a Hispanic person was interviewing some people who hold to a white supremacy ideology. These people were crass and cruel to the interviewer. I was appalled to hear the racist person begin to use the Bible to justify his hatred of every other race and his determination that only white people should live in America. At that point, I could not keep listening—I was too angry and upset. I was broken. This is wrong—so wrong!

This is not at all what the Bible is about. And it has nothing to do with who Jesus is and why he came. If anything, it is an insult to the God who made us, because this God has made us to reflect his image. And this God does not alienate or leave anyone out. We are the ones who separate or divide. We are the ones who reject him or one another, not the other way around.

It is no wonder more and more people are rejecting Christianity, seeing it as the cause of division rather than as the solution. Instead of being seen as a source of healing and unity, Jesus Christ is seen as someone to be rejected, and our voice as Christians as a voice to be silenced. When people look at the externals of Christianity, especially when modeled by broken human beings—it only makes sense to blame Christians for the issues facing our country and the world today.

But I believe rather than rejecting Christianity outright, we need to reeducate ourselves as to what it means to be a follower of Christ. We need to see Jesus Christ through the lens of the historic orthodox faith rather than the lens of social commentary and media frenzy. There is something substantial that can be missed when we do not look at Christ and Christianity in a way that takes into account the nature and being of the God who created humanity in his image to bear his likeness.

I don't profess to be a theologian. Nor am I an authority on social issues. But I am a fellow traveler on this journey who has been on both sides of the fence and who desperately longs to help others see the beauty and wonder of the life we were created to participate in. This is a life in which each and every person is fully valued, deeply loved, and entirely included. This is the life each of us was created for, and so we long for it deep down inside, and in our broken ways, we attempt to bring it into reality. We struggle and hurt one another in the process.

I pray perhaps this book might help at least one person grow in their understanding of who God is and who they are and what it means to make room for one another at the table. It consists of reflections, prayers, and scripture readings that can be a part of a person's daily devotional time. It's designed to help us rethink what it means to be human and participants in God's life and love.

Making room is not something that comes naturally, but it comes about as we live in the truth of our personhood as beloved children of God, and as we grow in our understanding of our common center in Jesus Christ and our inclusion in the divine life and love of the Father, Son, and Holy Spirit. May God bless you with patient understanding and grace as we journey together.

Overwhelm Me

The vacuum of my soul,
so empty of all that matters—
the callous indifference
to suffering and need,
the coldness toward those in pain
and the slave who should be freed.
How is it that love surrounds
and love consumes,
yet here I am,
left untouched,
indifferent to what is meant
to heal and comfort?
Lost and yet found,
cold and yet warmed
by the love of One who
would give me all?
Unrequited,
unaccepted,
cascading fountains of love and grace—
open the gates of my heart, dear Spirit,
that the King of Glory might come in,
that Abba might rest in comfort and ease,
and your Rivers of Life might
flow freely through the caverns,
crumbling them,
turning them into free-flowing streams
of living water
for lost souls.

1

Sharing the Same Earth
Ephesians 2:19–22

This morning, I am sitting in the office of the Social Security Administration, waiting to finish up some business regarding my mother's estate. As I sit in the hard plastic chair, I look around. People of all shapes, sizes, colors, and ages are waiting too, anxiously eying the board to see if they will be helped next.

It seems all of us waiting have a common concern this morning—having our particular need met by a government agency staffed with human beings like us. Each of us sitting here has our own unique story and our own special problem we need help with. We each want to be heard, and we each want to receive a solution to our own dilemma.

At a window nearby, a lady raises her voice. She is frustrated because she is having to state her personal affairs out loud because, she thinks, the agent won't read her paperwork. The agent continues to quietly help her, doing her best to understand the lady's situation. Unfortunately, there are laws and restrictions that prevent the agent from being able to do what the lady wants done, so the lady becomes angry and leaves.

When we are out in the midst of life, interacting with others, we come up against people who are very different from us. Our uniqueness meets up with their uniqueness. This can cause friction, misunderstandings, and pain. Or it can be an opportunity for one to help or strengthen or bless the other.

I recall a conversation I had last night where I was owning up to my tendency to be more spontaneous and easygoing than I am organized and controlled about my affairs. When I come up against someone who is very precise, disciplined, and organized, I can drive them crazy if I don't make some effort to be considerate of our differences. It is important to make room for one another and not to expect everyone to be the same as we are.

We can get so bent out of shape about our differences we miss the most important realization of all: even though we each have unique stories and ways of being, we also share a common humanity. We need to remember all of us come out of the same earth as Adam. The same elements that composed his body are those that exist in ours. The same Spirit who breathed life into him breathes life into each one of us. And the same God who created and sustains each of us came and lived as a human being just like each one of us.

As I sat last night and watched the preview of a new movie about Jesus when he was growing up, I was touched again by the realization of the humanity of Jesus as a young child. I have so many questions about what it was like for him: What was it like to be moved from one country to another as his family traveled from Egypt and settled in Nazareth? How was he able to grow up and come to a realization of who he was, while at the same time dealing with Satan's constant efforts to kill and destroy him? When did Jesus realize that he was not Joseph's child but was the Son of God? How did he feel when his stepfather passed away and he became the leader of his family in Joseph's place?

The battle Jesus fought in his humanity began at birth. I'm sure the angels were kept very busy watching over him as he grew up. When I think of all the children around the world today who lose their innocence or their lives on a daily basis due to people's inhumanity, it is a miracle indeed that Jesus, living in the Roman Empire, grew up to be the man he was. But having been a child, experiencing the things he experienced, Jesus could, with a warm and tender heart, hold children near and bless them when he was an adult. He knew what it was like to grow up in a dark, scary, and dangerous world.

I have a hard time believing that, as a child, Jesus was someone who took everything seriously and walked about preaching and praying all the time. I'm more inclined to believe he reveled in his and his heavenly Father's creation—running through the fields, wading in the streams, and chasing after the butterflies, just as my children did when they were little. I'm also inclined to believe Jesus enjoyed living, and so he laughed, joked with his friends, and played just like you and I do.

Talking and thinking about Jesus's humanity does not diminish him in any way. If anything, it makes him more amazing and worthy of our adoration and praise. Through Jesus, we can begin to find a commonality with God rather than just a separateness and uniqueness. Humanity is completely other than God, but God took on humanity in Jesus Christ so that we would be and are connected with God in the very core of our being—God in human flesh, transforming humanity from the inside out so that we can dwell forever with he who is completely other than us.

Jesus was not just a vague human being without distinction. He was born and raised in a specific culture and in a specific area of the world. He was a particular race and a particular gender. This does not mean he did not identify with others different than himself, but rather that no matter who we are in the specific way of our being, Jesus was that for us. He identified with us in our unique situation, in our unique time, place, and circumstance. Because he understood the context of his specific life, he understands the context of each of ours.

Unlike the agent sitting in the booth waiting to hear another person's concerns, Jesus is present and able to hear each and all of our concerns at every moment because he God. And he is present and able to understand and act in our best interest in every situation because he has experienced our humanity and shares it even now.

Wherever we are and in whatever situation we may find ourselves, we can trust we are not there all by ourselves. God has come through Christ and in the Spirit to live in human hearts. He is working to complete Christlikeness in each of us, because Christlikeness is our perfected, glorified humanity, which Christ lived out here on earth and which is poured out into each of us by the Holy Spirit.

We have nothing to fear, because whatever road we are on, Christ has walked it and will walk it with us all the way through to death and resurrection. We don't have to get anxious that God won't call our number in time. He's got each of us covered. He knows us intimately. We don't have to get upset if we aren't helped immediately—he's already working in our situation even though we may not see or recognize this is true. And we can trust he totally understands the details and will do what's best for us, no matter how things may appear to us at the moment.

Prayer

Holy Father, please grant we each might be of the same mind with one another according to Christ Jesus, so we all may with one voice glorify you. May we accept one another just as Christ also accepted us, so you might be glorified in us (Rom. 15:5–7). Thank you that before time began, you chose to adopt us as your children through your Son, Jesus Christ, and even when we were so terribly human and unlike you, you became like us so we could participate in your divine nature (Eph. 1:5–6; 2:4–7). Grant us the grace to love one another as you have loved us, through Jesus and by your Spirit. Amen.

2

Making Room
Galatians 3:26–28

I was looking at some of the responses to a recent event in Charlottesville and was appalled at the number of people who hold to the belief of the superiority of the white race. I understand from personal experience how insidious these lies can be. But what concerns me most is they are drawn from a misreading of the Bible. They twist the scriptures that, when read with integrity and spiritual wisdom, point us to the Christ who united all humanity with all its variety in his own person.

Indeed, Jesus laid the foundation in his life, death, resurrection, and ascension and in the sending of his Spirit. But he also calls us to participate in this reality that he created in himself. We can live in the truth of who we are in him or choose another path. Living in the truth of our humanity allows us to participate fully in the harmony and oneness of the Triune life, while choosing this other path creates what we see, hear, and experience today in these situations that involve violence, death, and suffering.

In contrast to the living God who is willing to lay himself down for another (and who did so), the evil one sets himself up as superior to others. He wants to elevate himself to a place where others must submit to him. He believes he is the one with the right understanding of how things really are, even though his logic is twisted and his motives are selfish and impure. Rather than assuming full responsibility for his shortcomings and misguided ways of living, he casts shadows onto others, making them at fault instead.

The error of this twisted thinking violates the oneness of the Trinity, where Father, Son, and Spirit live in a harmonious union in which each is unique, not the other, and yet is equal. As children made in this image, we as human beings were created to live in this same harmony as equals and yet as uniquely ourselves.

This oneness is not a forced sameness but a celebration of what each brings to the table—making room for one another. The reality is there are certain things we cannot bring to the table if there is to be room for everyone. These are things such as hate, greed, lust, pride, selfishness, and indifference.

Making room for all means we need an attitude of unselfishness, of humility, of service, and of giving. It requires a willingness to submit to another's way of doing things when we would rather use our own. Necessarily, there must be communication, encouragement, trust, and generosity—all things that are not the usual way most humans function. But these are the attributes of the God in whose image humans are made.

Unfortunately, our common way of creating harmony and oneness as humans is to create some form of sameness. We all must have the same clothes, the same behavior, or the same creed. We have to obey the same rules and follow the same leader. We must be the same color or the same ideology. But sameness eliminates the distinctness God created in the human race.

It is unfortunate the universal church has broken into so many facets. But even broken glass when it reflects the sun creates a pretty pattern on the wall. The oneness of love and harmony between people of all different faiths teaches people about the love of God for us as demonstrated in the gift of God's Son. It shows there is room for everyone at the table—we are all God's children and called to be members of the Body of Christ.

The variety within the universal church makes room for people with different needs, interests, and understandings of scripture. I have come to see that each person has a unique worship personality. Some of us connect best with God through the sacraments and through traditions. Others of us connect best with God and others through social service. Others of us find it is most meaningful to connect through the study of theology in a more intellectual way. God has made room for all in Christ to come into a meaningful relationship with him by his Spirit.

Those of us who follow Christ and who trust in him for salvation must never get to the place where we shut others out of their inclusion in God's love. Even though many do not see, or if they see and they choose to resist their inclusion in Christ, we must never assume in any way they are excluded from the invitation to share in God's life and love. There is room for each and every person at the table—there is a seat with their name on it waiting for them.

Nothing about any person is enough to exclude them from God's invitation to life. The color of their skin, the way they comb their hair (if they have any), their age, and not even their past is sufficient to prevent them from God's offer of grace and renewal in Jesus Christ. To divide up the human race into separate sections is to divide up Christ himself, and it must not be attempted.

Some may even be offended at the use of the name of Jesus Christ. To talk about everyone and God in the same breath is okay, but to mention Jesus Christ too is to become exclusive, they believe. But the whole point of the Christian faith is that all humanity, every race and ethnicity, has been swept up into Christ and thereby reconciled with God. Jesus Christ is not a point of separation between us—which is commonly believed and criticized—but is the point of unity between us all. He is our oneness. He is our harmony with one another.

In Christ's sending of his Spirit, he made it possible for us as humans to live together in ways we ordinarily cannot live. The Spirit changes hearts and minds and enables us to find our commonalities instead of focusing on our differences. When the Spirit goes to work and we are receptive, what normally would produce discord and division suddenly becomes harmonious. I have seen this firsthand in meetings that I thought were headed toward a free-for-all and ended up being experiences of compassion, repentance, and renewal. We all walked away newly joined together in a deep understanding and acceptance of one another.

But the path toward this type of oneness is necessarily, as Jesus Christ demonstrated for us, through death and resurrection. We need to die to our ungodly beliefs and our unhealthy ways of living and being. This is repentance. We need to rise in Christ to our new life he purchased for us and begin to make room for one another. We need to surrender our prejudices, our hate, and our evil and embrace the grace and love that are ours, while sharing it with each and every person we meet. This is faith. We turn from ourselves and turn to Christ. He is our oneness with God and each other in the Spirit.

Prayer

Abba, forgive us our hate, our prejudices, and all our failures to love. Forgive us for ever believing we were superior to another or more important than them. Grant us the grace to humble ourselves and make room for others, allowing them to be the people you created them to be in Christ Jesus. Give us courage and faith to resist anything that is not the truth about who you meant for us to be—to recognize evil for what it is and to bravely condemn and resist it, through Jesus our Lord and by your Spirit. Amen.

3

It's Just Not Who We Are
1 John 3:11

In the past few years, it has been brought to my mind over and over how our relationship with God is very much like that of an expectant mother, and our relationships with one another are very much like the cells in a human body. These are only analogies, and they have their shortcomings and flaws, but they provide windows into the human soul and our human existence.

This morning, I was reminded again how wonderful our bodies are. When something foreign enters our skin or enters our bodies, if we have a healthy immune system, the object or alien cell is immediately surrounded and attacked. The self-defense system within our human bodies is really amazing, but it has been known to even attack an unborn child if the antibodies are triggered by any antigens within the fetus. Obviously, this is not what antibodies were meant to do, but it can and does happen.

I pray God will help each of us to see ourselves as human beings held in the life and love of God, who upholds all things by the word of his power (Hebrews 1:3). And to see ourselves as sharers in Jesus Christ who has in his life, death, resurrection, and ascension made us participants in his very being, in his perfected humanity. For then we might begin to grasp—and I myself struggle to fully grasp this—sin and evil are alien to our true being. Any way of being that brings death instead of true life—the life

Jesus brought us into—the life and love that exist in the Father, Son, Spirit relations—is foreign to our true humanity.

Maybe it's time we begin to see our human proclivity to do what is evil and unhealthy from the point of view in which it is foreign to who we are. As the apostle Paul said, "If I am doing the very thing I do not want, I am no longer the one doing it, but sin which dwells in me" (Romans 7:20). That which is not you or me is what we find ourselves doing, even when we do not wish to do it. The desire to do what is life-giving and loving comes from God the Spirit, not our natural human flesh. When we are awakened to Christ in us, we find we want to do what creates harmony, joy, peace, and communion, not division, destruction, and death.

As humans, we have been joined with Christ in the hypostatic union of God and man, which he took on as the Word of God in human flesh. Jesus Christ took our broken humanity with him through the process of forging out a sinless life. He hauled us with him onto the cross, and with him we died the death we deserve to die. In Christ, as he rose from the grave, our humanity took on a new form. We do not live anymore in our human brokenness because God in Christ by his Spirit is awakening us to a new way of being that he has created—Christ in us, the hope of glory.

This new way of being is who we really are—this is our true humanity. Persons living in union and communion with the Father, Son, and Spirit, and with one another, are who we were created to be. To live in opposition to the perfected humanity that is found in Christ is to live in opposition to who we really are. We are the beloved children of Abba, sharers in the perfect relationship that exists between the Father and the Son in the Spirit. We are created to reflect and to live in this way of being—where our personhood is bound up in these inner relations in God and in loving relationship with one another.

So saying that, the elephant in the room is our proclivity to not live in the truth of who we are in Christ. In other words, there are a lot of things we think, say, and do that do not agree with who God has created us to be. We live with others and with God in ways that are self-centered, greedy, lustful, and broken and that bring death rather than life. We are created for life, not death. But we find so many ways to live in death, and sometimes we even imagine these wrong ways of living bring about life.

We walk in darkness, not realizing the light of God shines in us and through us. We even think following a bunch of rules, man-made or God-breathed, will give us life, forgetting that our real life is found in a person, Jesus Christ, and in our relationship with Abba through Jesus in the Spirit.

Our sinfulness is not our bad self, and our obedience to God and his ways is not our good self. We are not divided in two. We talk about bad people and good people, and I wonder whether we have ever considered exactly what it means to be a bad person or a good person. Exactly how much badness makes someone a bad person? And just how much goodness is needed to make someone good instead of bad?

What a revelation it can be when we realize we are all just a messy mixture of dark and light, of bad and good—we are all just very human. And as humans made in the image of God—warts and all—we are in Christ God's beloved and forgiven children. That's who we are!

Evil and the evil one are constantly seeking to destroy this new Body of Christ, as members in particular and as the corporate body. But the sins and sinful passions of our broken human flesh do not define us. Christ defines us. We are citizens of a new kingdom. And even though we don't always live like we belong to the kingdom of light, we do indeed belong there.

We've been given the glorious clothing of the kingdom of light to wear, and we have the privilege of living moment by moment in a close, personal relationship with the King of the kingdom right now. We have a new humanity we are able to fully participate in because the old is rapidly passing away—in fact, in Christ it is already gone.

Maybe it's time to quit listening to the lies and sitting in the dark, and awaken to the reality that we are already a part of a kingdom of light that has been in the works since before the beginning of time—an absolutely amazing kingdom in which righteousness dwells. Maybe it's time to embrace our true humanity.

Prayer

Lord Jesus, thank you for including us in your life with the Father by the Spirit. Thank you, Father, for drawing us up into the life and love between you and your Son in the Spirit. Enable us to turn a deaf ear to evil and the evil one, and to never again fear death, knowing we are hidden with Christ in you, God. Amen.

4

My Next of Kin
Matthew 12:46–50

When I was growing up, I believed I had very few relatives. I vaguely remember meeting my grandparents when I was little and a couple aunts and uncles and cousins on occasion, but the first time I recall meeting any significant number of my relations was when I was thirteen. Even then, I had no grasp of what it meant to be a part of an extended family with all the relational dynamics that go with it.

It wasn't until I began dating my husband-to-be and I married into his family that I began to experience what it is like to be a part of an extended family who lives within the confines of a small community. I remember on drives around the local area, they would point out a significant number of relations of theirs, whether near relations or shirttail relations, and they would tell me a little about each of these relatives' particular story. I was amazed to see who was related to whom and found myself quite nervous about possibly saying the wrong thing to the wrong person and creating a relational and community disaster in the process.

This type of community and family situation is much like the one Jesus grew up in. In Nazareth, no doubt, everyone knew everyone else, and their relationships were all intertwined as children grew up together, married, and had children who repeated the process. In his day, the family and continuation of the family line were of paramount importance. As the elder son, he had responsibilities to his family that he was expected to fulfill, and part of those involved having a sense of loyalty to his family and a commitment to their goals and expectations.

However, early on, beginning with his experience at the temple when he was twelve, we see Jesus beginning to differentiate between his relationship with his parents and his family and his relationship with his heavenly Father in the Spirit (Luke 2:41–32). He may have helped his mother with the wine supply issue at a local wedding, but he did so in such a way that reminded her and others of who he was as the Messiah (John 2:1–11). It must have been very hard for Mary to have her dear son draw this kind of a line in her relationship with him, but we see from early church history that eventually she understood and accepted the reality of who he really was.

Jesus's family was not always supportive of his ministry. In fact, at one point they tried to force him to come with them and said, in effect, "You are out of your mind!" Then there was the time when Jesus was speaking to the crowds, and his family came to see him. Someone told him they were outside waiting to speak with him, and he replied, "Who is my mother and who are my brothers?" Talk about a slap in the face!

But he wasn't trying to be insulting. Instead, he was making a point about the centrality of relationships to the Gospel—that we are all related to the Father through him in the Spirit. He is the Son of the heavenly Father, and those who live in the same *perichoretic*, mutually submissive, harmonic manner in which the Father and Son live in the Spirit, are his close relatives—his next of kin.

There are benefits to being Jesus's next of kin, you know. One of the significant reasons this is a good thing is because Jesus, being our next of kin due to sharing in our humanity, has the right of redemption.

The people of Israel understood what it meant to be a close kinsman with the right of redemption. That meant that when a person lost property due to debt or lack of heirs, the kinsman could and often would buy it back for them. It was not supposed to be allowed to go into anyone else's permanent possession; it was supposed to stay in the family. The story of Ruth gives a good description of what it was like to have a near relative redeem land that you lost due to not having heirs to give it to.

God created you and me to bear the image of the Father, Son, and

Spirit. We chose instead to define our own image of God and to follow our own way of being rather than reflecting the being of the living God. In many ways, we did, have, and still do damage to our inheritance as God's children. And we have incurred tremendous physical, mental, emotional, relational, and spiritual consequences as a result. Our debts to God are impossible to pay, both collectively and individually, especially since we refuse to quit incurring them.

It is instructive that God's way of entering into our impossible situation was to join us with himself by taking on our humanity. He became as closely related to us as he could possibly be. He became our nearest relative by sharing with us in our human existence—joining with his creation as a creature in human flesh (John 1:14; Heb. 2:11, 14–15, 17). He even did this to the extent that God "made Him who knew no sin to be sin on our behalf" (2 Cor. 5:12 NASB). Now that is taking his kinship to us seriously!

Being fully human as we are human does not in any way diminish Jesus's divinity. Rather, it is the tension of the two—that Jesus is both fully human and divine—that enables Jesus to do for us what we could not do for ourselves.

As your closest kinsman and mine, Jesus bought back our inheritance as God's adopted children. Running out to meet us as his prodigal children, in Jesus, the Father welcomes us home and is throwing us a great celebration. All that he has is ours in the gift of the Spirit—the indwelling Christ lives the life in us by the Spirit we were created to live as we respond to him in faith.

Some of us were not blessed with big, happy families to include us and to surround us with love. For many of us, being a part of our family of origin has not been a blessing or a joyful experience. The miracle of God's grace to us in Christ is that we are all included in God's family.

And God meant for those who believe to live together in such a way that they reflect the divine life and love, becoming a family of love and grace that embraces the lost, lonely, broken, and needy people who are looking for a home. If God can embrace and welcome broken, sinful humanity into his family by sharing in our broken, sinful flesh and living and dying for us, how can we do any less for others?

Perhaps it is time that we stop the "us and them" way of thinking and start practicing the reality formed in Christ that we are all "members of one another" (Eph. 4:25 NASB). We are all brothers and fathers, sisters and mothers in Christ, children of the Father, bound together in the Spirit. We are all kinfolk. Perhaps if we believed and behaved according to the truth of who we really are as God's beloved, adopted, and redeemed children, we might find the world becoming an entirely different place in which to live.

Prayer

Heavenly Father, thank you for giving us your Son to share in our humanity, to redeem us and bring us back into the right relationship with you, which you foreordained for us to have before time began. Forgive us that too often we ignore and hide ourselves away from you and from each other. Grant us the grace to live according to the truth: we are your beloved, redeemed children made to reflect your image, and we are all joined to one another in Jesus Christ. May we love others as you have loved us, through Jesus Christ and in your Spirit. Amen.

5

A Chance Meeting with My Sister
Matthew 25:34–40; Matthew 10:32–33

I was waiting in line at the post office the other day, waiting to pick up a letter I needed to sign for. The postal employee who was helping the people at the kiosks asked if anyone in line was picking up a package. I waved my little form in hopes he would help me out.

It was at this point I realized the lady behind me had waved her card too. But he told me to come first and then indicated that he would help her next. Behind me, I heard her make some rather loud remarks about "rednecks"—apparently the lady was upset because he didn't help her first.

As we moved over to the gentleman who was helping us, he asked if we were sisters. Before I could answer, the lady began a diatribe about how she was from a place in England, and she had lived in five states and hated Tennessee the most. She began to deride the people of Tennessee in a loud voice. I just tried to keep a friendly, calm demeanor, smiling at her when she looked at me. I wasn't sure how to respond, since she was clearly upset. The wise postal employee made himself scarce, and everyone in the line did their best to ignore the rude comments.

An older gentleman, when he finished at the counter, paused next to the lady and told her in a kind but firm voice he took offense at her insults of the fine people of Tennessee. She grabbed her bag and scurried away around me, trying to avoid him. She repeated her criticisms, and his parting words to her as he left were in essence, "If you don't like it here in Tennessee, you should leave." To this she replied, "If I could afford to, I would."

She and I returned to our waiting positions, and that inner voice we don't always want to listen to said to me, "You know, she is your sister—in Christ." I felt like I wanted to say something to her about this, but the words stuck in my throat.

At this point, the postal employee called the lady over for her letter and apologized to her for the wait. She grabbed her letter and left with whatever dignity she could muster. She was still clearly upset.

"I'm sorry," he said to me. "I thought you two were related. You looked like you were sisters."

"No," I replied. "I don't know her. I've never met her before."

I signed for the letter from the funeral home and left. As I stepped out of the rear door of the post office, I looked across the parking lot. She was sitting in her car, and she was crying. The irony that struck me at that moment was that this woman who was so rude to me and to everyone else was the same woman who I had let go first when it was clearly my right of way into the post office driveway.

In spite of all she had said and done, my heart went out to her. She was clearly in distress, but my presence and knowledge of that fact seemed to only be making things worse.

I left, but that whole conversation stuck in my mind. I joked about it later, telling people that I was finally a real Tennessean now—a true redneck apparently. But what kept echoing in my mind were those phrases: "She is your sister—in Christ" and "I don't know her."

Later on as I pondered this experience, I thought of those three conversations Peter had when Jesus was on trial. Three times he denied Christ: "I don't even know the man," he said. This one, Jesus, who said Peter was his brother and his friend, Peter refused even to acknowledge (Matt. 26:72).

Jesus said when we welcome another person in love and compassion, we are welcoming him. To call this lady my sister was to acknowledge Jesus Christ and all he has done and is doing to bind all humanity to himself in his human flesh through his life, death, resurrection, and ascension. She is as Christ is to me—bone of my bone, flesh of my flesh—we are one in Jesus Christ.

To deny that relationship in essence is to deny Christ. To reject her or to refuse to have compassion for her in her need is to close my heart to the Spirit's call to love her with the love of the Father for his Son.

This was just an everyday happening in my life. Nothing to get too excited about or beat myself up about. But through the lens of eternity, it can be seen in an entirely new way.

Here, in view of the kingdom of God, is a fellow citizen—someone who may or may not know that their place of birth is in the Son—a birthplace they share with all humanity. As a sister to this person, I have the opportunity—no, the challenge—to acquaint her with the truth about her beginnings, her real family, the place where she truly belongs. Why should I be silent about so great a thing?

This is the good news we share. We are all one in Christ Jesus—God has claimed us as his own in spite of our brokenness and sin. He has said that he would not be God without us—and he made sure of that by giving us himself in the Son and in the Spirit. Each person we meet is truly and completely loved by God and forgiven, whether they deserve it or not—and most of the time, if they are like me, they don't deserve it.

More and more, God is leading me to pray a simple prayer as I go about my daily life asking God to show me what he has for me to do or say in each moment. As my friend Steve calls them, I ask God for "spiritual conversations." I ask God to set me up and to give me the words to say and the courage and wisdom to say them in the right time and in the right way.

Our confession of Christ is in our common humanity we share with him and with one another. We cannot and must not stand aloof from one another, even though there may be a fear in our hearts that the person we are helping may harm or hurt us. We can be wise and have healthy boundaries with people, but at the same time, God calls us to tear down our barriers and to truly love one another from the heart in the same way he loves us through his Son, Jesus Christ. May we be faithful in so doing.

Prayer

Holy Father, thank you for not rejecting us but rather calling us your very own. Thank you, Jesus; you call us your brothers and sisters and your friends. Thank you, Holy Spirit, for being our Paraclete—the one who comes alongside us to share in every sorrow, joy, struggle, and celebration. Thank you, God; you are faithful and true, and you have made us all to be one with you and each other, and to live together forever in love. Through Jesus and in your Spirit, we pray. Amen.

6

Our Unifying Distinctions
1 Corinthians 12:18–20

Recently at Good News Fellowship, we wrestled in our group discussions and in our sermons with some things we as humans commonly believe about God that are not according to the truth revealed to us in the person and presence of the Lord Jesus Christ. One of the lies that seems to raise its ugly head from one generation to another is the belief we are, in our uniqueness as a particular color, race, or ethnicity, God's chosen people. This lie puts us in direct opposition to those who are "not like us" and creates division and even hostility between us.

What we don't seem to realize is God never meant for our differences to divide us, but rather to bind us closer together. What makes us distinctly unique is meant to be an important part of a complete whole that celebrates the wonder and glory of our divine God who is Father, Son, and Holy Spirit.

God himself in his being teaches us it is our uniqueness that binds us together. It is never meant to divide us. God as Father, Son, and Spirit has distinctions, but these distinctions in God's being do not cause division. Rather, they describe the interrelations in God's being. The Father is not the Son, and the Son is not the Father. Rather the Father is the Father of the Son—this is their oneness in the Spirit. The Spirit is not the Father, nor is he the Son, but he is the one who is the Spirit of the Father and the Spirit of the Son.

I remember hearing and being taught as a child that I, as someone of light complexion, was part of a special group of people chosen by God, and those of darker hue were somehow part of the human race who were cursed with Cain. This teaching created a sense of cognitive dissonance in me because I had friends in school of much darker hue than me, and they did not seem to be any different from me. How is it they could be less than or inferior to me when they were actually the same as me?

Since that time, God has taken me on a journey of learning and healing in which I have come to have warm and meaningful relationships with people of many different races and ethnicities. I have come to see the truth—we are all one body made up of different members. We each have a role to play in the common humanity of God's creation.

Indeed, I believe the apostle Paul hit on something really important when he began to talk about the different parts within the body of Christ (1 Cor. 12). I believe this concept extends beyond the walls of the church. Our common humanity is made up of all different sorts of people, and none of us really looks exactly the same, though some of us may look similar to one another.

This morning, it occurred to me again that if there were no such thing as brain cells, how would any of us think? If there were no nerve cells, how would our brains communicate with our bodies? If there were no skin cells, how would our muscles and organs stay where they belong, protected and held in place? These cells are each unique to one another and even have variances in between them, but each is necessary to the whole; the body would not function properly if any of them were missing or were not properly fulfilling their function.

There is a reason we are the way we are. There is a beauty in the human race that is expressed in all its different hues and distinctions. These differences were meant to create joy and celebration as we share them with one another. Instead, we allow them to create fear, hate, and hostility against one another. These distinctions were meant to create a greater, more blessed whole, but we have allowed them to divide us and to cause us to destroy one another.

We forget or ignore the reality that God's Son, who was completely other than us, took on our humanity—joined himself to us permanently—so we could share in his being. Jesus Christ became sin for us so we could become the righteousness of God in him. We share in Christ's being because he took that very thing that has divided us and destroyed our relationship and used it to bind us to himself with cords of love.

God was not willing to be God without us. He did not allow whatever differences between us and him—which are vast and unmeasurable—to cause us to be permanently separated from him. He did not consider himself to be above us, but rather, he humbled himself, setting aside the privileges of his divinity to join us in our broken humanity (Phil. 2:5–11). He humbled himself, even to the point of allowing us to crucify him. What we did to try to permanently separate ourselves from God, he used to bind us to himself forever. Such an amazing love!

In binding us all to himself with cords of love in Jesus Christ, God also bound us to one another. We all share in the common humanity of Jesus Christ, and there are no longer any divisions between us. We are all one in Christ Jesus. Whatever we may artificially place between us is now caught up in Christ's humanity and reconciled with God, and we in Christ are all reconciled with one another. There may be distinctions, but in Christ we are all one.

God is calling to each of us to respond to his Spirit as he works to bring this oneness to full expression in our individual and common humanity. The Spirit calls to you and to me to respond not only to our reconciliation to God but also to our reconciliation to one another in Christ. There are to be no divisions between us. Whatever distinctions may exist are meant to be a cause for giving praise, glory, and honor to God for his wisdom and goodness, not a cause for fear, hate, and hostility between us.

May we turn from, or repent of, our human proclivity for racial and ethnic superiority and inferiority and stop yielding to the evil one's efforts to divide us and so to destroy us. Let us, rather, build one another up in love. Let us look for reasons to share and celebrate our differences and distinctions and to make them ways in which we can come together to create a stronger, whole humanity.

Instead of allowing our distinctions and differences to cause fear, distrust, hate, and hostility, may we actively work to make them the very thing that binds us to one another. Sometimes this may require the same path Jesus trod—through death and resurrection—but the result will be something we will not experience otherwise: a taste of the kingdom of God here on earth as a reflection of the love that exists in our Triune God as Father, Son, and Spirit in heaven.

Prayer

Dear Abba, forgive us for all the ways we create division and discord in our world. Forgive us for the ways we demean one another and the arrogant and prideful ways we have of living and being. Grant us the humility and dignity of our true humanity in Christ Jesus. May we, from this day forward, always treat others with the same respect, kindness, and graciousness with which you have treated us, through Jesus our Lord, and by your Spirit. Amen.

7

The "Righteous" Life
James 1:19–20

As many of the members of our congregation know, our pastoral team uses the Revised Common Lectionary as a resource in preparing our sermons each week. This helps us to keep in step with the Christian calendar and enables us to cover a large portion of the biblical text as the year goes by.

One Sunday, I hoped to preach on one of the passages listed in the lectionary—in particular, a passage in James 5. Several times during my morning commute to my second job, I listened to the book of James being read aloud. I don't know if you ever have this happen when you read God's Word, but something just jumped out at me as the reader was speaking.

Perhaps I was just in a Trinitarian frame of mind. I don't know. But what struck me was James was expending a lot of energy talking about what it meant to live righteously. Over and over, he described what the godly life looks like and what it doesn't look like. And it all had to do with relationships.

The relational God, when he lives in us by the Spirit and we are responding in faith to his work in our hearts and minds, moves us to live in ways that build and reflect healthy relationships. It seems to me, when righteousness is discussed in terms of "right relationship," it can be described in just the way James described it.

For example, when James says a person who does not guard his or her tongue is not practicing true religion (James 1:26), he is showing how what we say or do not say reflects what is going on in our hearts and minds. Later he reminds us when we are living out of the truth of who we are in Christ—the spring of living water—what we say will reflect Christ's wisdom. When we are living out of the acrid, putrid water of our flesh, we will say things that are abusive and reflect a heart full of jealousy and selfish ambition (James 3:9–18).

Obviously, what we say and how we say it directly impacts our relationships with God and with other people. Speaking out of the abundance of a heart full of evil motives and desires will not achieve the right relationships we wish to have with God and others—it will not produce the righteousness of God.

James says in another place, "the anger of man does not achieve the righteousness of God" (James 1:19 NASB). When we think in terms of relationships and the love that goes on within the Triune God, this can seem like a no-brainer. Our flashes of human anger where we are triggered and we blow up at the people around us—usually people we love and care for—do not build relationships but fracture and harm them.

When we are in tune with God's heart and mind though, living out of the spring of living water who dwells within us, we will be quick to hear, slow to speak, and slow to anger—all of which build relationships and do not destroy them. When we look at the human life Jesus lived on this earth, we see this very thing occurring in all his relationships. This is the way of being of the God who lives in and with us through Jesus and in his Spirit. This is what Jesus, by the Spirit, puts into our hearts and minds.

This is the "wisdom from above" described by James: "But the wisdom from above is first pure, then peaceable, gentle, reasonable, full of mercy and good fruits, unwavering, without hypocrisy. And the seed whose fruit is righteousness is sown in peace by those who make peace" (James 3:17–18 NASB). The fruit or result of living out of the truth of who we are in Jesus is right relationships with God and others. How we live with one another—which spring we draw from—determines the seeds that are planted in our relationships and the fruit that is borne as time goes by.

This puts me in mind of a friend whose supervisor is rude, disrespectful, and controlling. He creates an unhealthy work environment for those who are unfortunate enough to have to be his employees. And it never occurs to him the poor work performance and rotten attitudes of some of his employees may be the result of the way he treats them. The fruit of what he is sowing certainly isn't right relationships!

Broken, fractured marriages result when spouses live out of the rottenness of their human flesh rather than out of the life-giving spring of living water available to them by the Holy Spirit. Even so, putting two people together in close proximity means there will be misunderstandings, inadvertent hurts, and thoughtless acts. This is why we need something or someone beyond us interceding between us in all these situations.

Christ living in us enables us to weather relational difficulties and to resolve impossible relational schisms. Time and again, I have seen and experienced the healing that comes when we turn to Christ in the midst of these difficult situations and begin living out the truth of who we are as God's children. Prayer and seeking God's will and grace are fundamental to the success of any relationship. Why?

Because of the reality that Christ is the mediator in any and every relationship. He is both the mediator between God and human, and he is the mediator between each of us as humans, because in him, God and humanity are joined as one. In all our relationships, he is the center and source of our oneness with each other.

This is the ultimate indicative or basis for every imperative or command we read in James. Because we are connected at the core of our being with the one Jesus Christ who is connected with all others, we have every reason and ability to live in right relationship with God and others. In Jesus Christ, we also find we have—by the gift of his Spirit—the strength beyond our strength, the wisdom from above, to relate properly with God and others when our flesh is calling us to do otherwise.

God never meant for us to be estranged from him or any other person but for each and all of us to live as one with him and one another. And it was always his desire to share himself with us so we could. And this beautiful thing happened when God came to earth and took on our humanity as an infant born that glorious night in Bethlehem. The God of peace gave us the

Prince of Peace so we could live forever at peace with him and one another. Shalom!

Prayer

Abba, thank you for the gift of your Son and your Spirit by whom we may have peace with you and one another. May we live out of the abundance of your life in us so we may live in the truth of who we are in you. Through Jesus, our Lord, and by your Spirit. Amen.

8

Being Human—Who Am I?
2 Samuel 7:18

A while back, I was loaned a DVD set of a space western that contains all the necessary attributes of a western drama—knockdown drag-out fights, shootouts, ambushes, a train robbery, and much more.

It tells the human story in a postmodern way, so there is much to be gathered from the human interactions. But it is a much more graphic style of storytelling than I prefer, and I think some may even find it offensive. (It's definitely not kid friendly, so I'm not recommending it.)

The creepiest and most horrific part, I thought, is the role given to the humans who are so twisted and depraved they torture, abuse, and cannibalize any humans they come near. They haunt the outer reaches of the galaxy where people are settling new planets and there is very little law and order.

In one piece, the crew of the spaceship comes upon another spaceship whose travelers have been ambushed, savagely brutalized, and killed by these creatures. As they try to decide what to do in the situation, they begin to argue over whether or not these savages were even human. Could people who did the things they did to other humans even be considered human beings?

Indeed, I wondered as I watched this, at what point do human beings cease to be human beings? And what would it take for a person to cease being the human being he or she was meant to be? Is there a description that we can go by to decide who is and who isn't truly human?

If we were to be honest with ourselves, we would have to admit we all have times and places where we are less than what we were meant to be. We are inhumane to one another and sometimes even to ourselves.

The early church wrestled with the question of who God is and who Jesus and the Holy Spirit are in relationship with God. Why were these important questions?

These were important questions because who God is as the Father, Jesus Christ, and the Holy Spirit determines who we are. This is because we are created in God's image. God, who is three persons in one being and who lives in an eternal relationship of mutual love and respect, defines our personhood. He is the description of the God we were created to reflect.

This is why the doctrine of the Trinity is so essential to our humanity. God, who is Father, Son, and Spirit, is one being but in three distinctive persons. We cannot separate the Father from the Son or from the Spirit—they are inseparable. The Son is not the Father, is not the Spirit, and yet they are one. Unity, uniqueness, and equality—this describes the Trinity. This transcendent mystery is the basis for our humanity.

When we fail to acknowledge or submit to the reality that God defines us and our humanity and how we are to live in relationship with others—in equality, oneness, mutual love and respect for one another's personhood—this is when we cease to be truly human. When we try to live out of sync with who we were created to be, then we begin being inhumane—not human—not who or what we were meant to be. And so we end up creating misery for ourselves and others.

The problem is this is the human condition. We're just that way. Somehow, from the beginning, we have chosen to define ourselves by our own rules, deciding for ourselves what is good and what is bad. And we have sought to eliminate, as much as possible, any memory of there being a God who defines us. The tree of the knowledge of good and evil is a tree we eat of on an almost daily basis—we, in our arrogance, have sought to redefine what it means to be a human being.

What we need is some genuine humility in the presence of the one who made us and gives us each day all we need for life and godliness. It is in acknowledging our inhumanity, our pride and arrogance, that we will truly begin to find ourselves.

God has already resolved the issue with our broken humanity. He came into our human existence, took on our human flesh, and, in Jesus Christ, lived out a truly human existence—one he has given to each of us through the Holy Spirit as we welcome him.

Will there always be those who refuse to live out the new, transformed humanity given to us in Jesus Christ? Yes, for we are given the freedom to refuse God's gift of love and grace. And, yes, there will come a day when God will draw a line and affirm our choice, even if it is to refuse and to live apart from the grace God has offered us in his Son. God will allow us to live in the darkness of our consequences forever, if that is our choice.

Meanwhile, it would be worth our while to begin practicing some humility and grace in our relationships with God and one another. It would be a good thing for us to express some genuine love and respect toward each and every person in our life, even though they may be behaving in some very not human ways. We would find our lives much different if we began living out of the divine definition of who we are, rather than the one we have picked out for ourselves.

Prayer

Holy God, forgive us our arrogance in trying to define you and ourselves according to our limited and often misguided human reason and wisdom. Forgive us for the inhumane ways with which we treat one another and you. Thank you that ultimately you are the one who defines us and who has restored our true humanity in Jesus Christ. Thank you for warmly welcoming us into a personal relationship with you in Jesus Christ through the Spirit. In his name we pray. Amen.

9

The Whole Message
Acts 5:19–20; John 6:63

I recall when I was growing up being told by ministers the true Gospel preached by Jesus was about the kingdom of God that would be inaugurated when Jesus came back to earth after the great tribulation had occurred. I remember these men ridiculed the messages taught by mainstream Christian churches, saying that the gospel preached by such churches wasn't the true gospel but a false, misleading one.

Since that time, the Spirit has been gracious and has helped me see there was a lot of misleading information I took in and believed, which I needed to reexamine. And when I did reexamine the Gospel message Jesus and his disciples preached, I found that it wasn't at all what I was being told it was. In fact, it was something entirely different.

For example, in Acts 4, Peter and John were put into prison because they were "teaching the people and proclaiming in Jesus the resurrection from the dead" (Acts 4:2 NASB). Later when the council threatened them and told them not to preach in Jesus's name any longer, they replied, "Whether it is right in the sight of God to give heed to you rather than to God, you be the judge; for we cannot stop speaking about what we have seen and heard" (Acts 4:19–20 NASB). In other words, they were telling people what they had witnessed in Jesus's life, death, and resurrection, not about some new kingdom, or some laws they were to live by, or some days they were to keep.

The apostle Paul, after his encounter with Jesus on the road to

Damascus, "immediately ... began to proclaim Jesus in the synagogues, saying, 'He is the Son of God'" (Acts 9:20 NASB). His message had to do with who Jesus was and what he did when he was here on earth. And whenever Paul made a defense in regard to why he was doing the ministry he was doing, he told who Jesus was and what he did but also what Jesus had done in Paul's life and how Paul had been changed by his encounter with Jesus. The gospel he shared had to do with the life of Jesus, and how the living Jesus impacted his own life in a powerful way.

When Stephen was taken before the council and was accused of speaking against the temple and the law, his defense did not involve preaching about some soon-coming king or kingdom. His defense involved telling God's story—the story of how God worked with Abraham and his descendants to bring them into relationship with himself, and how they had over and over rejected his love and grace, and how in that same way they had rejected his Son Jesus Christ. Stephen died because he told God's story—the story of God's life with Israel and the Spirit's work to bring Israel into a loving, obedient relationship with their covenant God through his Son Jesus Christ (Acts 7).

When the high priest and the Sadducees put the apostles in prison out of jealousy because the crowds were being healed and delivered from evil spirits, we read an angel came and released them from prison. Then the angel told them, "Go, stand and speak to the people in the temple the whole message of this Life" (Acts 5:20 NASB). And so they did what they were told. And they were found again in the temple preaching the "whole message of this Life." The high priest and the Sadducees were upset not only because they were preaching about Jesus, his death and resurrection, but they were also angry because the power behind that message was being experienced through people being healed and delivered.

When Peter was sent for by Cornelius, he obeyed the will of the Spirit. Cornelius and his household were prepared to hear the Word of the Lord from Peter—he was going to preach the message they needed to hear. And when he spoke, he began with God's acceptance of all people but then told them about the life, death, and resurrection of Jesus Christ. And he finished his message by telling them all who believe in Jesus Christ receive forgiveness of sins. As they listened to this message, God poured out his Holy Spirit on Cornelius and his household—this was a transformational event in the life of the church.

Jesus called certain people to be eyewitnesses of his whole human existence. They had seen, heard, and touched him. They knew he was both human and divine. They would truthfully tell "the whole message of this Life" they had experienced firsthand. As the apostle John wrote: "What was from the beginning, what we have heard, what we have seen with our eyes, what we have looked at and touched with our hands, concerning the Word of Life—and the life was manifested, and we have seen and testify and proclaim to you the eternal life, which was with the Father and was manifested to us—what we have seen and heard we proclaim to you also, so that you too may have fellowship with us; and indeed our fellowship is with the Father, and with His Son Jesus Christ" (1 John 1:1–3 NASB).

So, part of this message that includes the life, death, and resurrection of Jesus Christ is the good news that we all have forgiveness available to us through him. We learn in this message about who Jesus is—the Son of God and the Son of man. We learn that in Jesus Christ we all died and rose again. This message includes God's story—his life with humanity, with Israel and with his disciples, and with the church through the ages—as God has interacted with, healed and restored, and delivered people by his Holy Spirit. This "whole message of this Life" is so much more than just a message about some king and a kingdom or some rules to live by.

This "whole message of this Life" is life-giving because it is the Spirit who gives the words life. The good news of who Jesus is and what he has done and is doing is transformational because, in Christ, we are all forgiven and are given new life. In Jesus Christ, we have a hope and a future, no matter what we may be going through right now.

Just as Jesus has become a part of our daily life, he becomes a natural part of our conversation with others. The early persecuted church "who had been scattered went about preaching [bringing the good news of] the word" (Acts 8:2 NASB). Sharing the good news of Jesus became a part of their everyday life, which they took with them everywhere they went, no matter their circumstances. As we go about our daily lives, we tell others about who Jesus is and what he has done and is doing. We share with others the ongoing story of what God is doing to transform our lives and the world we are living in.

Even though we have not personally lived with Jesus or personally witnessed his crucifixion and resurrection, we each have our own story of how Jesus met with us and transformed our lives by his indwelling Spirit and his intervention in our lives. We can tell how our lives intersected with God's life through Jesus and by his Spirit. All God asks us to do is to tell the story, to tell the "whole message of this Life." Jesus and his Spirit will do the rest.

Prayer

Holy Father, I pray by your Spirit you will enable us to share with others the "whole message" of your love for humanity expressed to us in the gift of your Son and your Holy Spirit. Empower us to speak with courage and conviction as we tell your story and our story, and the story of Jesus and his transforming and healing power through his life, death, and resurrection. I pray more and more people will come to know and receive the forgiveness available to them through Jesus Christ. In his name, we pray. Amen.

10

The Curses and the Ten Commandments

Deuteronomy 27:26; Mark 12:29–31

This past year, I've been starting out my day by reading a chapter from the Old Testament and a chapter from the New Testament. One morning, I was reading chapter 27 in the book of Deuteronomy. Here, Moses instructed the people about something they were to do when they entered the Promised Land. They were to divide the people up, with six tribes standing on Mount Gerizim and six tribes standing on Mount Ebal. Then the Levites were to recite curses, and all the people were to respond with "Amen" to each curse.

Something occurred to me as I was reading this. It was something I had never paid close attention to when I read it before. And it really bugged me—enough that I had to stop and think seriously about it for a while.

If I were to ask you what many traditional and fundamentalist Christians have posted in their house or office somewhere, what would you say? I was in someone's office the other day, and there it was, in bold print, so everyone who came in couldn't miss it. Many Christians insist the Ten Commandments are the trademark measurement of goodness and badness and are what matters most to God in our relationship with him, so they post them where they and others can see them.

That being the case, I was stunned to see that nowhere in this list of sins these curses were for were the breaking of the Ten Commandments specifically listed (Deut. 27:14–26). A person would be cursed for "misleading a blind person on the road" but not for taking God's name in vain. Or people were cursed for "striking their neighbor in secret" but not for killing their neighbor.

If the Ten Commandments were so important for the people to be keeping, why weren't they listed with the curses? And I found it interesting, in the same respect, that each of these things listed had to do with proper relationships between people, both in the family and in the community. The last one in the list was a summary statement pronouncing a curse on anyone who did not uphold the words of the law.

The blessings and curses that were to be regularly recited had to do with whether or not Israel as a nation trusted in God alone and was faithful to their covenant relationship with him. The blessing pronounced in Deuteronomy 28 is God's response to Israel properly participating in their covenant of love with him by living in communion with him.

In both of these cases, the Ten Commandments were supplanted to some extent, or shall I say, surpassed by, the greater law of covenant love. Our relationships with God and with each other are what really matter in the end. The consequence of living for ourselves and not living in communion and godly love with one another and God is well described in this listing of curses. And the blessings that come with living in the communion of the Holy Spirit with one another is clear to see as well. It explains why Jesus, when asked, said the most important commandment is to love God with one's whole heart, soul, mind, and being, and the second is just like it—to love our neighbor as ourselves.

Instead of seeing the law as a list of dos and don'ts that separate good people from bad people, we see the law as an expression of what it looks like to live in loving relationship with God and each other. The simplicity of this is expressed in the New American Standard Version when it says the people were to confirm the words of the law *by the way in which they lived* (Deut. 27:26). We confirm our love relationship with God and each other by the way we treat God and each other and by what goes on in our hearts and minds in each moment of each day as we interact with the world around us.

Going on beyond this, we are told by the apostle Paul, "Christ redeemed us from the curse of the Law, having become a curse for us …" (Gal. 3:13 NASB). So even our shortcomings in living out a relationship of love with God and each other are covered by our Savior. The prophetic word of Isaiah to Israel was that God would author a new covenant in which he said he would "put My law within them and on their heart I will write it; and I will be their God, and they shall be My people" (Jer. 31:33 NASB). This is reflected on by the author of Hebrews, who explains the gift of God is the internal eternal law of God, Jesus Christ, who has joined himself with humanity and who stands in our place as both the lawgiver and the law keeper.

Now, I'm not against people posting the Ten Commandments in places as a reminder of how to treat God and each other. This can be a good thing. But it is easy to hold to this external expression of goodness and badness by which we judge one another and to totally miss the mystery of godliness—Christ in us, the hope of glory. It is Christ who defines us, who lives his life in us and through us by his Holy Spirit. It is God who plants within us the heart, soul, and mind to love him and each other from the core of our being with his very own love, planted within us through Jesus Christ in the Spirit.

How often I have encountered people who are very busy with the externals of Christianity but who are also vindictive, hateful, spiteful, and even cruel—because the law has become a dividing point of goodness and badness between them and other people. They have missed the one who gives life and offers us an intimate relationship with himself through Christ in the communion of the Holy Spirit.

They are eating of the tree of good and evil and have missed entirely the tree of life offered us in Jesus's life, death, resurrection, and ascension. This seems to me to be the worst possible thing that could happen to anyone. And all these curses described in Deuteronomy cannot begin to describe what it's like to live out one's life in rejection of the one who is our life, our love, our obedience, and our peace. This seems to me to describe in many ways what a personal Gehenna looks like.

Prayer

Dearest God, thank you for giving us your Son so we can live in loving relationship with you and each other. Thank you for your precious Spirit, who opens our eyes and minds and hearts to see Jesus Christ living within, and who makes us receptive to the truth and life he is. Grant us the grace to seek life in Jesus Christ, instead of seeking to be our own gods and to live independently of you and each other. We trust you will finish your work in our hearts, minds, and lives, through Jesus Christ. Amen.

11

The Divine Aggressor
Matthew 16:18

The last thing I would ever want to do would be to make God look like he is an evil monster looking for opportunities to destroy you or me because of our badness. It seems our ways of looking at God and thinking about him do enough of this without my helping them along.

But we do need to understand God isn't just a nice, feel-good sort of person all the time. Just because he is loving and compassionate doesn't mean there aren't things he really truly hates. Indeed, God abhors and vehemently opposes anything that mars the beauty he created you and me to reflect. He is passionately opposed to those things that keep us from being the image bearers of God he created us to be.

This passion of God—this "wrath" of God—is behind all he has done in sending his Son to live, die, rise, and ascend on our behalf, and behind his sending of his Spirit to dwell in human hearts. This passion of God has driven him from before time to ensure what he began in us would be completed through Christ and in his Spirit.

There is one who has opposed God from the beginning and who, with his followers, seeks to destroy God's work and to undermine his efforts in renewing all things. The adversary opposes all that is good and holy. He labors constantly in an effort to turn human beings against the God who made them, sustains them, and redeemed them. Any effort we make to trust in and obey the God who is Father, Son, and Spirit is resisted and thwarted by the evil one.

In many worldviews, good and evil are seen as equal opposites that must be kept in a constant state of balance for people to be able to exist in harmony and peace. The balance I see being kept in the divine life and love is not of the balance between good and evil but the perfect harmony and oneness of the Trinity in their equality and diversity. Evil in this worldview only exists as that which opposes the Trinity, and it is allowed to exist only because of the freedom of will given to those who are created by God.

God summarily dealt with evil and all who oppose him in our cosmos by taking on our humanity and dealing with it from the inside out. He was very aggressive in tackling the issue of our broken humanity and the efforts of the evil one. In Jesus Christ, God conquered death and Satan and gave us all a new life in Christ, which is ours through the Spirit.

The message we find in Revelation and elsewhere is Satan and death are defeated foes, and we have nothing to fear. In fact, God sent his Spirit, and he is systematically penetrating this world with his very life through his gathering of believers (which we call the church) who are the body of Christ. There is a finality about the destruction of Satan, his demons, and evil, as well as death. As far as God is concerned, it is already over with. All that's left is the mopping up. What we experience today of evil and death and suffering is just a temporary blip in the radar, and in time, it will all be gone.

Today in Christ and by the Spirit, the kingdom of God has already been established in our world, just as one day it will be fully established when Jesus Christ returns in glory. In this way we live in and participate in the already, but not yet, of God's kingdom. God has invited believers specifically to participate with him in the expansion of his renewal of all things to fill the whole cosmos. He is inviting those who follow Christ, and indeed all humanity, to join with him as he aggressively intervenes to bring healing, hope, and restoration in many people's lives all over the world.

We forget sometimes we are at war. We forget our Jesus is a mighty warrior fighting on behalf of all that is just, holy, right, and good. And he has invited us to go with him into battle against all his foes—all who oppose the glory he created human beings to reflect.

God is not impotent against the forces of evil at work in this world. But he has invited us to share in the battle, and he has reasons for allowing things to happen the way they do. As the commander in chief who died at the hands of humanity so humanity could be saved, he has a way of dealing with evil that often seems out of sync with our reality. This is why it is so important we follow the lead of his Spirit and grow in our knowledge of who Christ is and who we are in him. God's ways are not our ways, and his thoughts are not our thoughts.

The bottom line is to trust him—to believe Abba loves you and me so much that not only did he send his Son, Jesus, to free us from sin and death, but he is also sending his Spirit to bring to fruition all Jesus forged into our humanity in his life, death, resurrection, and ascension. Thankfully, Jesus even took care of our need for faith by accomplishing in himself our perfect response of love toward Abba. We are held, we are loved, and we are Abba's beloved children, and God will accept nothing less than this for you and for me. This is his passion, and Jesus will see it is realized by his Spirit as we turn to him in faith.

Prayer

Thank you, Abba, for your great love and faithfulness toward all you created. Thank you for giving us the freedom to choose and the privilege of mirroring your glory and goodness. Thank you for allowing us to participate in all you are doing to renew what you created and you sustain. We trust you to finish what you have begun in us through your Son and by your Spirit. In your name, we pray. Amen.

12

The Battle against Despair
Psalm 146:5

I recall a conversation I had a while back with a beautiful lady who has seen the struggles and difficulties of life. She had recently experienced the cruelty of unjustly losing her livelihood after having worked very hard to finally have her own home and to pay off all her bills. When she was finally starting to see some light in her dark life, she was knocked down again.

In the midst of this situation, the one thing she needed, she said, was to have some glimmer of hope. She needed to be able to believe there was a good reason to go through another day, to try one more time to do things in an honorable and ethical way in the midst of a culture that told her to take the easy route of dependency, addiction, and sloth.

To tell her to keep believing, to insist that she try one more time, was not enough. She had reached the end of her resources—there wasn't anything left inside to carry her, and there wasn't anything left outside in her life to lift her up. She felt all alone, forgotten, unloved, and unwanted. She felt a deep sense of despair. Nothing could help her.

Or so she thought. It was in the midst of this place she encountered the living Lord.

How Christ comes to meet us in the midst of our despair and darkness is unique to each of us. He met his people of Israel in a time when they despaired of ever hearing from God again—a time when they were held in the grip of a pagan government that disrespected their heritage and their God. And he came to them in a form they never expected—a tiny, helpless infant laid in a manger by a common carpenter and his bride.

One of the ways Christ came to this lady in despair was in the people of faith he began to place in her life. These particular people began to share life with her, expressing God's love for her in various tangible ways. They offered her what they could and pointed her toward others who could help her.

They did not always do what she expected. They did not pay all her bills or take care of her problems the way she wanted them to. But they did provide her with love and concern and prayer. They did provide her with the means to better her life and to grow as a human being into greater Christlikeness. It turns out that through them and through the Word of God, they gave her what she needed most—hope in the midst of her despair. They introduced her to Jesus Christ.

Christ is our hope in the midst of despair. He is that divine Word from the Father of Lights who entered our humanity and joined us in the midst of our human depravity and our broken world. He even "became sin for us," taking on that very thing that keeps us in our despair and brokenness. And he died our death and rose from the dead, giving each of us a new life, a hope in the midst of despair.

In sending the Holy Spirit, God through Christ made a way for us to begin to experience the kingdom life even now in the midst of our broken and sinful world. We are able to interact with God in a real way through our union with God in Christ and our communion with God and one another in the Spirit. Through Christ and by the Spirit, we are able to experience a living, ongoing relationship with God himself, coming to hear and understand the living Word of God personally and having God's way of being written on our hearts and minds.

This means Christ becomes and is a real part of our day-to-day existence. As we respond to his nudges by the Holy Spirit, we come to experience healing, hope, and change in our lives. Things don't always get better immediately as far as our circumstances may go, but somehow this doesn't matter so much to us anymore.

In the midst of our struggles and dark places, God begins to shed his light. We begin to have a new perspective. We begin to see and experience possibilities where there were none before. God brings us into relationships that are healing, helpful, and restorative. He begins to change our lives.

But God doesn't do this all by himself. He calls us to participate with him in this transformation. We can continue to wallow in despair if we wish and deny the real grace God offers us in the midst of our suffering and grief. We can cling to our darkness if we wish—God allows us to do that. But he calls us out of it and offers us himself, through Christ and by his Spirit, as a means of lifting us up and transferring us from darkness and despair into light and life.

As participants in God's light and life, we need to be sensitive to the work the Spirit is doing to draw others out of despair and darkness. We are called by God to share with others the Word of life we have been given. We can give them a real hope in the midst of despair when we introduce them to Jesus Christ and show them God's real love and compassion.

We come into their lives the way God in Christ entered ours—humble, insignificant, and truly human. We share the mundane parts of our existence with them, along with the relationship we have with our heavenly Father through Christ his Son and by his Spirit. We give what we can to help them become the children of God they were created to be, so they can also be full participants in God's love and life. This is our participation in what Jesus is doing in the world today.

Offering someone just a little bit of hope may seem trivial. We may think we have to accomplish great things in the world or become well known for our Christian faith and piety. But the simple gift of hope can be life transforming and healing in more ways than we could ever imagine. Just ask someone who has received it.

Prayer

Lord, thank you for coming into our world and joining us in our humanity and our brokenness and for healing us from the inside out.

Thank you that you offer each of us hope in the midst of our despair. Do not leave us here in our dark places, but please come to us and lift us up into your arms of love and life. Make us compassionate to others who need the gift of hope, through Jesus and by your Spirit. Amen.

13

Something from Nothing
Romans 4:17b; Hebrews 11:3

When my children were very little, I was often called upon as their mom to rescue them from a serious dilemma, such as fixing their tricycle, putting the head or arm back on their doll, or saving them from the neighbor's scary dog. All these issues were well within my ability as their mother to resolve. But on occasion, they asked me to do something that was beyond my capacity as a human being, such as bringing their deceased pet fish back to life. In these cases, I found myself having to explain to them that I just could not do it. This they could not understand, because in their eyes, Mom could do anything!

Ah, the disillusionment of youth when they find out their mom or dad is just like themselves—imperfect and insufficient to meet their every need! But this is a life lesson we are all faced with at some point. To promote another human being to the place that God reserves for himself alone is risky business indeed. And it often can be destructive to the one who is placed on a pedestal. It is essential to our mental, emotional, spiritual, and even physical health to recognize and admit we are incapable of perfection, of sustaining ourselves or others, or of creating something out of nothing. Only one being has that ability and prerogative.

The testimony of the Christian scriptures is that God, who existed apart from and before time as Father, Son, and Spirit, created all that we know today out of nothing. He did this to share with created others, unlike himself yet like himself, all the blessings of the love and life of his being. Since the beginning of time, we as human beings have questioned God's love and goodwill toward us, and so we have found many ways to put barriers between us and the God who made us. We have attempted to play his role in the universe as well as our own. And the results continue to be tragic.

But God said, "No!" to all we have done in this regard. He has affirmed his intention we all share in the life and love of Father, Son, and Spirit as he ordained in the beginning. It is for this reason that in the fullness of time, he came himself as the Word in the person of Jesus Christ. He came as God in human flesh so he might completely express his love toward us. God is making something out of nothing, and he will finish what he has begun. The proof of this lies in the glorified human form of Jesus Christ, who lived, died, and rose again to live forever at God's right hand in glory.

So, when we get discouraged by life and our inadequacies, when we see the impossibilities of life, when we can only see evil and destruction and despair—this is the time to remember the God who made all things out of nothing. He is not done yet. He will finish what he has begun. He will bring perfection out of our imperfection, wholeness out of our brokenness. He is our Redeemer and will redeem all things.

As we daily surrender our inadequacies, failures, sorrows, and weaknesses to him and embrace the risen Christ in their stead, we will experience the transformation of our deadness into life in him. This is the promise we have in Jesus—to share in and participate in his perfected human life both now and forever. It doesn't depend on us; it depends completely on him. We are reminded of this as we participate in communion, eating the bread and drinking the wine in remembrance of him. God knows the end from the beginning, and he has declared our salvation in Jesus Christ. And he will not fail us in this. Believe it or not.

Prayer

Dear God, thank you so much for your perfect gift in Jesus Christ and the precious Spirit who lives in us to bring to completion the perfected life of your Son in each of us. We trust you to finish what you have started in us. Our hope and our faith are fully in you and not in ourselves. Open our eyes to see you and know you for the loving, faithful, gracious God you truly are. In Jesus's name. Amen.

14

Stop Hiding and Start Finding
John 17:3, 25–26; John 7:28–29

I was thinking about how, when they were little, my children loved to play the game of hide-and-seek in the dark. Although they loved to play outside, some of the best fun we had as a family was playing hide-and-seek in the dark in our old two-story house with all its closets and hidey-holes.

It was always a challenge to try to find a place to hide where you could not be found. So often we reverted to subterfuge to confuse whoever was looking so they would not think to look where we were hiding. They wouldn't think to look under the clothes in the closet—so that's where we would hide. They wouldn't think to look in the bathtub, so that's where we hid, and we'd sneak out at the end so they wouldn't know where we successfully hid and find us the next time.

It seems in the game of hide-and-seek, it was always a problem to get someone to be "it," to be the finder. We all loved to hide, but who wanted to do the finding, especially when someone might jump out of a dark corner and scare us half to death?

I think in many ways this game of hide-and-seek has translated into adulthood in the context of our relationships. In our complex society today, I believe too many of us are busy hiding—behind our jobs, our weight, our addictions, our toys, and many other things—and very few of us are doing the looking. Building relationships that are deep and lasting is fast becoming a lost art in the midst of our technology-driven culture.

It is no wonder marriage has lost its appeal to so many people. Marriage requires intimate knowing, transparency, and vulnerability—all which are very difficult to do when a person is trying to hide. It necessitates both parties being willing to be "it" all the time, and this takes effort, time, commitment, humility, and grace.

As I think about this, I'm reminded of the God who created all things and placed within us the heart that loves the game of hide-and-seek. He plays "it" all the time and doesn't seem to mind. In fact, he came himself as the Word into our time and space to live among us. He found us, experienced our human existence, and opened us up to life with him. In Christ, he comes out of hiding and lets us find him. And he invites us into a transparent relationship with him, where each of us is fully known and loved. He flips the light on and calls us to come out of hiding and be fully exposed.

But coming out of hiding, being authentic and real with each other and with God, is a scary business. This is why God gives us grace. He invites us to trust in his love for us—that he won't jump out of a dark corner and shout, "Boo!" He invites us to live openly with him—moment by moment in real relationship with him. He calls us to be real, to truly be who he created us to be, without any fear he's going to sneak up behind us and frighten us.

And God calls us to live in community with one another in the same way. He brings us together in the unity of the Holy Spirit in love relationships where each person is able to be authentic and transparent, without fear of rejection, criticism, or betrayal. These are relationships or spiritual communities where the Holy Spirit is actively working, where each person is not trying to control, manipulate, use, or abuse the other but where there is mutual submission, humility, service, cooperation, and respect instead.

All this takes effort. And it requires a commitment to stop hiding and to be willing to play "it" for a while—or to a least allow Jesus to be "it" in our place. To know and be known is essential to our humanity—it's what we're created for. We need to have relationships with God and with each other that are healthy, transparent, and committed.

Jesus said that true life, life that is everlasting, is life in relationship—knowing and being known. He has included us in his relationship with the Father in the Holy Spirit. And he has bound us together with one another in his humanity, serving as the divine mediator between each of us, and between us and God. There is a home base, or shall I say, a person, where we are fully known and fully loved, and even our best efforts at hiding are futile. Maybe it's time to call the game over, flip on the lights, and have a group hug. "All outs, all in free!"

Prayer

I'm so thankful, God, you know us completely, inside and out, and still love and care for us. You have revealed yourself to us in Jesus, and you do not hide yourself from us, except in those ways that are appropriate to your divine glory. Thank you for including us in your eternal love relationship of the Father with the Son in the Spirit. Grant us the grace to truly love one another in the way you have loved and made yourself known to us in Jesus. In his name, we pray. Amen.

15

Putting New Wine in This Old Wineskin
Matthew 9:17; Luke 5:37–39

A while back, I spent several hours in the emergency room because my heart was in atrial defibrillation and would not go back to a regular rhythm until I had been given several medications. Having an event like this in my life has given me an opportunity to simply appreciate the moments I have left, as well as the relationships God has blessed me with over the years.

Going through this has also helped me once again to face the over-fifty reality that I'm getting older and my health is not what it used to be. Genetics, lifestyle consequences, you name it—it all adds up to I can't do everything I used to be able to do. My mind and my will may want to do certain things, but my body just can't take it anymore, whether I like it or not.

When I worked at the care center, I used to laugh with the seniors about this. We'd agree together: just like a fine wine, we don't get older—we get better and more refined with age. It's not that getting older is so bad; it's just having to live with the body that goes with it—it just doesn't work like it used to, and that's no fun.

Sometime in the midst of my musings over my forced rest from any stress or exertion, my morning reading included the passage in Matthew 9 where Jesus talked about not patching an old piece of clothing with new cloth, and not putting new wine into old wineskins. For some reason, this really stuck out in my mind, probably because our lectionary passage for the upcoming Sunday was the story about Jesus turning water into wine.

Jesus had this deal about wine. I think it's pretty funny Jesus would do an "in your face" type of move like turning the water used for ritual washing into wine for drinking. How like him!

And he didn't just make enough for the day's meal. He made more than one hundred gallons! There could be some serious inebriation going on with that amount of wine at the wedding. But that didn't seem to matter to him.

Changing water used for ritual washing into wine to drink—there are a lot of ramifications to what he did in this simple miracle. When he talked about the importance of not putting new wine into old wineskins, he was talking about something similar, but totally different as well. The first things most commentators stress about both is Jesus was pointing out the reality that the old way of the Jewish temple worship was to be superseded by the living Messiah, who would be both our sacrificial lamb and our high priest. The old way of approaching God and worshiping him was being replaced with the new way of the ministry of the Spirit through Christ.

But it struck me this week there was a lot more going on here than just the removal of an old sacrificial system through the coming of the Messiah. Indeed, Jesus did a lot more than just create a new way of worshiping God. What he did in sharing our humanity, dying our death, and rising again was so much more than that.

We learn in Ephesians 1 and elsewhere that, before time, God intended humanity to share his life and love as his adopted children. But as we were, we could not hold the majesty of the life of the Trinity within us in the way that God wanted us to. We could not share in the divine life the way God intended us to.

Truly, God holds all things, and nothing exists outside of him. But there was a lack in our human capacity to relate to and grasp the spiritual realities we were created to exist within. We could only see ourselves as alienated from God and unworthy of his love. In many ways, our humanity was like those old wineskins. If God would have tried to pour into us the fullness of his glory and love, would we not have been broken? For surely God offered us his life, but we rejected it.

Jesus, in coming into our humanity, dying, and rising again, created for all of us a new wineskin and then sent his Holy Spirit to dwell in human hearts. What amazing love God has! He did exactly what it took so we could share in the divine life and love!

Now, just as Jesus said, we have the incredible gift of the indwelling Father and Son in the Spirit available to us—a new wine that can be poured into these old wineskins, which have been made new so they could contain this new wine. Instead of those old clothes that are patched and worn, God gave us new wedding clothes.

And here I am, back at the wedding again, where there's an overabundance of wine. Surely God's Spirit is limitless, and God has poured out on us the tremendous precious gift of his Spirit, who brings all God's blessings into full expression in us and in our world, as we participate actively in the divine life and love through faith. Drink in of this wonderful luxury—God's presence in us and with us at every moment, as we are held in union with God through Christ and experience loving communion with God and one another in the Spirit. That's some wedding!

Prayer

Thank you, Father, for inviting all of us to the wedding of your Son to his beautiful bride and for creating in Christ a new humanity to be filled with your divine presence in the Spirit. How wonderful we all may live each moment in anticipation of the day when we can sit at this wedding feast in glory, but thank you also, for even now we sit in glory with you through Christ in the Spirit and can drink in of that heady, glorious wine of eternity each and every moment of every day. In your name, Father, Son, and Spirit. Amen.

16

Rain in the Desert
Genesis 3:8–9

I remember a brief visit to the Arizona desert. The setting sun was painting the sky with brilliant colors. The saguaros and Joshua trees were silhouetted against it, and the air was crisp and dry. The desert was beautiful, but it was dry and parched. The only thing that would have made it even more beautiful, that would really have made it come alive, was rain.

Sometimes, like the desert, we may feel dry and parched. We feel an inner emptiness that nags at us, which we really can't quite put our finger on. We try to avoid dealing with it, so we cram ourselves and our lives full of all kinds of stuff, none of which truly fills that emptiness. Our life may have a stunning beauty and be full of an abundance of blessings, but nothing quite takes away that nagging feeling of thirst.

The sad thing is we can be doing all kinds of things for God and still feel this way. This is because we have forgotten who we are and what we were created for. We weren't created to do things for God but to do all things with God.

Adam and Eve were placed in the Garden of Eden to tend and keep it and to be fruitful. And God walked with them in the garden—sharing life with them as they went along. God did not just put them in the garden and then walk away and say, "Take care of it. It's all up to you now. You've got to get it right or else."

But he did give them a choice—the same choice he gives us. A choice between life on our own—choosing for ourselves what is good and evil—or true life, life in communion with him forever, trusting him in every situation. Even when Adam and Eve made the wrong choice, God intervened and promised them evil would not have the last word. Their failure was not the end of the story. It was redeemed in Christ.

Because Christ took on our human flesh and lived, died, and rose from the grave in union with us, all of life is a participation in God's Triune life and love. We can try to live life as though we are here on earth all by ourselves, tackling everything on our own. (Our track record with that hasn't been the greatest.) Or we can live life in an intimate relationship with God, moment by moment through Christ in the Spirit.

Through Christ, God sent his Spirit so that we could share in his life. We are free to ignore the tree of life, the Spirit, if we wish and continue to hide away from God. Worse yet, we can declare ourselves aligned with God and with Christ as our Savior and yet live as though it's all up to us. Either way, we end up making demands on other people they cannot fill. And we live with an inner dryness we try to stuff with all kinds of things that never quite fill the emptiness.

Instead we can choose to live our lives as a participation in Christ's life, believing all of life is taken up in Christ. Whatever we are doing at the moment, we do walking in the Spirit and in union with Christ—this is our communion with God in Christ by the Spirit. This is the *perichoretic* life of the Father, Son, and Spirit—making room for one another. God has made room for us in his life. We make room for God in ours. We make room for others in ours as well. We live gratefully in God's true freedom based in love, in a warm, loving relationship with God and each other.

This means we live, moment by moment, with an awareness of God's presence. We begin to tune into the presence and power of God's Spirit. We make some effort to listen to the Word of God and the promptings of his Spirit. We begin to make room for God in our hearts, our minds, and our lives. And this requires slowing down and walking at God's speed, not our own speed.

Every act of life, no matter how trivial, is not an unusual thing for God—he is not surprised. He already knows all about us. He knows us intimately. Nothing is hidden from him, no matter how good we are at hiding it.

He wants to share all of life with us just as we would with a spouse, a best friend, a lover, a brother, or a sister. God wants to do all of life with us, not just the parts we get right. That's why he gives us his unconditional love and acceptance—his grace. And he loves us so much that he's not going to leave us where we are—he's going to grow us up to reflect the perfect image of himself, Jesus Christ. He's going to work to heal us and make us whole. He's going to transform us.

When we feel that nagging inner thirst, we need to ask ourselves—am I doing life on my own again? Where's God in all this? Who is God for me in this moment, in this situation? Am I doing life for God or for myself? Or am I doing life with God—together with him in joyful companionship and friendship?

Whenever we find ourselves in that dry spot where we've started going the wrong direction, all God asks of us is to turn around. He beckons to us, "Come—join me in my life and my work! Share life with me! You don't need to do this all by yourself." And he runs down the road to meet us and embrace us. Because he's always expectantly looking for us to join him. Let's not keep him waiting.

Prayer

Holy God, thank you so much that we don't have to do life all on our own. Thank you for your real, intimate presence with us and in us by your Holy Spirit. Forgive us our proclivity to live life our way, on our own, without you. Grant us the grace to make room for you in our lives, our hearts and minds, and to live each moment in an intimate relationship with you. Fill our thirsty souls with your real presence—we long for you. We've lived too long in this desert place without you. We praise and thank you for your faithful love in Jesus. Amen.

17

What Does It Mean to Repent and Believe?
Ephesians 3:20–21

Have you ever had that experience where you were praying about something, asking God to move in some situation, and when things actually began to improve, you were still in the "I have to do something to fix this" mode? It reminds me of the story of Peter being released by the angels from prison, going to find the brethren who were praying for him, but when he knocked on the door, no one believed it was him (Acts 5:1–19).

I have no doubt that we *want* God to intervene and to answer our prayers. But do we really *expect* him to? Do we really believe God exists and he wants to and will intervene in our lives and circumstances?

In this culture that is so heavily wrapped around science and proving things according to empirical data, I think it is interesting that we even have scientific studies that prove praying for the sick actually works. But why do scientific studies of such a thing? Why do we have to prove prayer works and is helpful?

I wonder if there is a deep inner longing in each of us to experience in a real way something outside of our human existence, something beyond ourselves that is more than we could ever be and is lovingly inclined toward us and willing to help us when we are in need. And yet if there is such a being or force, we most certainly don't want them to interfere with us or to tell us what to do. We want all the benefits of such a relationship but none of the responsibilities.

We want to have help when we need it, to have success and good health and all of the glitz and glamour of a blessed life, but we surely don't want anyone to dictate to us how to go about obtaining it or living it. We like to do life on our own, to deal with our problems our own way, and then to blame God or karma when things don't turn out like we expect.

And prayer seems to be that guilt thing we think maybe we ought to do more of now and again. We know prayer would be good to do when we're in crisis and we don't know where else to turn. But what do we know and believe about the God to whom we are praying? Do we really believe he cares and he will give us an answer? Or are we essentially atheists or humanists in our prayer life?

There is something fundamentally wrong here, and I believe it has to do with what we believe about God. First off, it is wonderful if we can get it through our minds and hearts that God is *real* and God *loves us*. Period. He did, he does, and he will love us unconditionally, no matter where, when, or how we find ourselves—even in the midst of the stupid stuff we do.

And God gives us grace—total, unconditional forgiveness. But in the midst of that forgiveness and acceptance is the unspoken reality that we need this forgiveness. Karl Barth in his *Church Dogmatics* reminds his readers that inherent in our receiving forgiveness is the acknowledgment of our need for it. God offers through receiving his gift of grace the opportunity to experience a change of mind and heart. This is called repentance and faith.

One of the ways we need to experience repentance and faith is in this area of our view of God, so we see him as a loving, merciful Lord who answers our requests for help and succor. We need to come to see God as a person who cares about every facet of our life and who is ready and willing to help.

But along with that understanding of who God is needs to come an appreciation and respect for the right he has as a living Lord to personify for us who we are to be as human beings. The lives we live ought to reflect the God in whose image we are made, and Jesus Christ as the true image bearer of God is that image (Hebrews 1:3). How we think, behave, and speak ought to correspond directly to the thinking, behavior, and speech of Jesus Christ as it is revealed to us through the Holy Spirit and in the holy scriptures. We need to acknowledge that sometimes the mess we are in is our fault and we need to change.

Don't get me wrong. God's not hovering over us waiting for some reason to slap us silly since he knows we're going to mess up. No. He loves us, and he hates anything that will mess up our understanding and experience of his love. He hates anything that will mar the beauty of his image in us. He longs for us to fully experience the love, joy, and peace of a life like his, which is whole, blessed, and healthy.

He wants us to see him for who he really is and to live accordingly. And prayer becomes a part of this reality in our lives. Because we know him as a God who loves and forgives us, we want to know him better. Knowing him better means we begin to see things about ourselves that need to be changed. So, we go back to him, secure in his forgiveness and love. And our relationship with God grows deeper as we are continually drawn to deeper levels of repentance and faith.

Drawing closer to God means we see more areas of our being and life that do not reflect his glory. So, we surrender to God in those areas rather than resisting him. Prayer then is just a natural part of our relationship with God—he shares himself with us, we share ourselves with him, he responds, we respond; throughout our lives it goes on. But we need to be careful not to allow any part of our being or life to be a place where God is not allowed to have a say in how we think, speak, or live.

I'm not talking about rules. I'm talking about a real relationship with someone who wants to do more for us than we could ever think of or ask him for. I mean being so close to God in our hearts and minds we don't want to wound him in any way by the things we think, say, or do. We seek only to give full expression of God's glory in and through us in every way possible.

This is tough, and it is countercultural. It goes against our natural human inclinations, and it definitely stands in opposition to all that is dark and evil and opposes the will and purposes of God.

But God stands with us and promises us he will never leave us or forsake us. He is committed to our becoming all we were meant to be as his adopted children in Christ and by his Spirit. And he won't quit until he is done. We can count on that.

Prayer

Holy God, please forgive us our wrong-headed views and thoughts of you. Grant us the ability to see you with new eyes and hearts. Open up to us a new understanding of who you are and how your heart toward us is only good and loving. Grant us repentance and faith, through Jesus Christ and in your Spirit. Amen.

18

Learning to Lament
Isaiah 53:2b–8

One Sunday, I began my section of the service by reading portions of some news stories about mass murders both here in American and in the world outside our borders. These stories effectively illustrated the brokenness of our humanity—the natural inclination of the human heart toward evil. One of the hardest things for us to admit as human beings is our proclivity toward harming ourselves and others.

It is easy to read these stories and say to ourselves, "I would never do anything like that! Not ever!" And yet we find ourselves yelling at our children, crucifying their self-esteem, because they leave the milk out all night or drop our favorite dishes and break them.

Listening to these stories may awaken a lot of feelings inside of us—feelings we often do our best to ignore, bury, or dismiss by the flurry of a busy life. These feelings of devastation or grief at such great loss, or raging anger at such injustice, can overwhelm us so much we find refuge in our addictions or bury ourselves in endless new forms of entertainment. Or we may lash out in a violent rage, thereby perpetuating injustice and evil rather than ending it. Facing the reality of our broken humanity and our own proclivity to harm others and to be unjust is hard work and requires a lot of fortitude.

I believe it would be a good thing if we each could learn and practice what is essentially a spiritual discipline. We need to learn to lament—to learn how to listen to the cry of our heart against evil, pain, and destruction, and to allow it to speak to us about who God is and who we are in the midst of our brokenness, and to motivate us to participate in God's work in the world to right such wrongs. Learning to lament can teach us how to encounter God and his light in the midst of the very darkness that seeks to destroy us.

When we are made aware of or experience a devastating loss, a horrendous injustice, or a crushing inhumanity, we need to pause and pay attention to what is happening in our hearts. We need to lament. We need to stay in this place long enough to ask God, "How do you feel about this? Holy Spirit, enable me to see, to hear, and to know your heart about this right now."

The reason we lament is to realize what is going in our own hearts and how it mirrors what is going on in the heart of God. What you feel about these losses, injustices, and inhumane events—your pain, your sorrow, your anger, your desire to avenge the wrongs—this is a reflection of God's heart.

And yet how God deals with these things and has dealt with them is different from how we as humans believe things should be handled. And so, we do not recognize God is at work in these situations. He is at work—he does not ignore any of this. But how do we know this is true?

First, I believe we have an answer in the prophetic word of Isaiah where he spoke about the suffering servant who was to come and who did come in the person of Jesus Christ. Look at what he wrote:

> He has no stately form or majesty that we should look upon Him, nor appearance that we should be attracted to Him. He was despised and forsaken of men, a man of sorrows and acquainted with grief; and like one from whom men hide their face he was despised, and we did not esteem Him. Surely our griefs He Himself bore, and our sorrows He carried; yet we ourselves esteemed Him stricken, smitten of God, and afflicted. (Isa. 53:2b–4 NASB)

We hear Isaiah telling us about the anointed one, who was just like you and me but was despised by the people around him. Often people say that God is the one who inflicted pain and suffering on his Son, but in reality, it was we as human beings who tortured and crucified Jesus Christ unjustly. Going on:

> But He was pierced through for our transgressions, he was crushed for our iniquities; the chastening for our well-being fell upon Him, and by His scourging we are healed. All of us like sheep have gone astray, each of us has turned to his own way; but the LORD has caused the iniquity of us all to fall on Him. He was oppressed and He was afflicted, yet He did not open His mouth; like a lamb that is led to slaughter, and like a sheep that is silent before its shearers, so He did not open His mouth. By oppression and judgment He was taken away; and as for His generation, who considered that He was cut off out of the land of the living for the transgression of my people, to whom the stroke was due? (Isa. 53:5–8 NASB)

The Creator and Sustainer of all life and every human being took on our humanity and allowed us to pour out on him all our prejudice, anger, hate, fear, rebellion, and all those inner drives that divide us. Jesus walked as a lamb to the slaughter, silent, with no refusal to anything done to him. He took on himself God's passion against sin by receiving from us all our hate, anger, fear, prejudice, and rebellion and becoming sin for us, in our place.

God's heart about all these things we are talking about is compassion; he enters into our brokenness and sin and suffering and shares it. He became the Word in human flesh (*sarx*), the broken part of us, and became sin for us so that we might become the righteousness of God in him—*righteousness* meaning we are brought into *right relationship with God and one another*.

The meeting place between every human being on earth is Christ, the one who is fully God and fully man, who tore down every wall between us in his incarnational life, suffering, death, resurrection, and ascension. God has forged a oneness between all of us in his Son, which is unbreakable—yet we experience none of it as long as we deny this reality.

God has already entered into our darkness, fully received our rage against him in his rejection, crucifixion, and death, and has already translated us, taken us out of that darkness into his marvelous light, into his kingdom of light. God has already paved the way to our healing and wholeness as human beings by pouring out his passion against all that mars our true humanity, all our divisions, all those things that *separate* us, by taking it upon himself in his Son.

One of the basic lies of the evil one since the beginning has been that you are separated from God and each other. And unfortunately, we believe him.

God is one—a unity, a whole, in which each are equal yet diverse. God is love—dwelling in a perichoretic relationship of mutual indwelling. This is the God in whose image we were created. We were created to live in this way—to love God and to love our neighbor. This is *who we are*.

God knew beforehand that in our humanity alone we would never live together in this way, even though it was what we were created for. Abba planned from before time began to send his Son to take on our humanity, knowing his Son would take upon himself the worst of all we are as humans. But God knew in doing so his Son would, by the love and grace of all he is, perfect and transform our humanity.

All that Christ forged into our humanity in his life on earth—his suffering, his crucifixion, death, resurrection, and ascension—is ours today and is being worked out in this world by the Holy Spirit. The Spirit is at work right now bringing this perfected humanity and the kingdom life of God into real expression in the world in the hearts and lives of particular people. We see the Spirit most active in the universal body of Christ where there is true perichoretic love—we know Christ's disciples *by their love for one another* (John 13:25).

You and I participate in the Spirit's transforming work in the world as we respond in faith to his work in our hearts and lives. If you know what God's heart is about all these things that are happening today—that God's heart is full of compassion and concern and a desire to bring people together, and to help heal relationships—then you know how to participate in what God is doing in the world today by his Spirit to make things better.

God doesn't do everything alone; he includes us in what he's doing.

The reason things aren't getting better but are getting worse may be because we are quenching the Spirit of God; we are closing our hearts to God's power and will being activated in our circumstances. Sometimes we don't listen to and obey the promptings of the Spirit to pray, or to say a kind word, or to help those in need, or to encourage those who are suffering. Sometimes we refuse to listen to the prompting of the Spirit, who is asking us to forgive a wrong, to go make things right with someone we are estranged from. Sometimes we refuse to hear God's call on our hearts to intervene in a difficult situation and to act as a mediator.

And sometimes we refuse to set aside our own prejudices and expectations, and our own animosity against someone of a different culture, race, ethnic group, or belief system. We hold onto our grudges, our resentments, our anger, our sense of injustice instead of obeying God's command to forgive. We feel we are owed something better.

But I ask you: what could anyone possibly owe us that would even come close to what we owe Abba after all we did to his Son when Jesus came to offer us life and we killed him? Nothing. Nothing at all.

Thankfully, though, God does not leave us in our pain, our brokenness, anger, resentment, and sorrow. No, he meets us there. Our failure to live in love with God and each other is the very place God entered into in Christ. He meets us in our failure to live in love and says to you and to me, *I am yours and you are mine.*

It is God's nature in our humanity by the Spirit that brings us together and joins us at our core humanity. Abba has declared his Word to us: "My adopted children, the whole human race, are diverse, yet equal, and are to live *united*, as a whole, as one body. They are *never to be separated* from me or each other." Abba has sent his Son, the living Word, into our humanity to join us with himself and one another through the hypostatic union between God and man. Individually by faith in Christ, we as humans are united with God in Jesus Christ by the Spirit.

Abba has poured out his Spirit on all flesh so we might live together in holy communion both now and forever. The Spirit works out into all our relationships with God and one another this true reality of our hypostatic union with God in Christ. This is the true reality of who you are and who I am. You are an adopted child of Abba, the Father, and he has bound you to himself in his Son, Jesus Christ, and to one another. The person next to you is also an adopted child. And the person you just can't stand is also an adopted child, whether you like it or not, and whether they know it or not.

The Spirit's work is to bring each person to an understanding and awareness of this reality of who they really are. You and I participate in that work as we respond to the Spirit's inspiration to bring healing, renewal, restoration, forgiveness, understanding, and reconciliation. God has given us the ministry of reconciliation, for he has reconciled all things to himself in Christ Jesus. And by the Spirit, we participate in Christ's ministry in the world.

Let us, through lamenting, face the truth of our brokenness and the horror of our depravity. May we see that Jesus meets us there in that very place with his mercy and grace. May we understand that Jesus has bound us together with God in himself so we are *never to be separated* ever again. We are called to live in *union* with God and one another forever in the Spirit. And may we indeed find, by the Spirit who dwells in us, we are reconciled to God and one another, so we have the heart of Abba and Jesus to make amends, to create community, to restore relationships with God and each other, and so we are able to experience true spiritual communion with God and one another.

The power of lament is the power of the Gospel. The power of lament is the power of the Spirit to call us back to the truth of who we are in Christ, and the reality of our reconciliation to God and one another in the finished work of Christ. Let us respond to God's call upon our hearts to be reconciled. As we live in this reality of who we really are, as God's adopted children, in our differences, our equality, and our unity in Christ, we will find our world being transformed, healed, and renewed.

Prayer

Thank you, Abba, for your heart of love and grace, which you share with us through your Son and by your Spirit. May your heart of love and grace, which you place within us, find full expression in every area of our lives and in the world in which we live. Through Jesus and by your Spirit, we pray and we work to participate fully in all you are doing to bring healing, renewal, reconciliation, and transformation to this world. Amen.

19

Leaving It All for Love
Luke 18:28–30; John 15:12–14

Many years ago, I packed everything I owned in a U-Haul truck and left my Southern California bungalow for the hills of rural southeast Iowa. It was quite a cultural shock for someone who had grown up in the suburbs of Los Angeles. Over the years, people have often asked me what in the world made me do this.

At the time, it just seemed the logical and right thing to do. I was in love and had married an Iowa farmer. To leave my home, my family, my friends, my job, and all that was familiar to me seemed to be only a little thing in the face of building a new life based on love.

One of the stories many of us had to read in high school was Shakespeare's *Romeo and Juliet*. In this classic story of love and tragedy, we find the age-old question asked, "What would I do for love?" It is a question many of us face in our day-to-day lives as we interact with family, friends, and our community. What exactly are we willing to do in the name of love?

Throughout his ministry, Jesus engaged his disciples in conversations that challenged them with this very same question. He walked up to Matthew as he collected the taxes and said to him, "Follow me." And Matthew dropped everything and followed him. Jesus went to John and James and said to them, "Come, follow me, and I will make you fishers of men." And they left it all and followed him.

Making Room

Throughout this ministry, the disciples kept being faced with the question, am I really ready and willing to leave all behind and follow Jesus? At one point, they reminded Jesus of all they had given up to follow him and asked what they were going to get out of the deal. Jesus said they would receive abundant rewards in the world to come, as well as receive some rewards now. But the greatest gift they would receive through it all would be eternal life in relationship with the God who loved and cared for them.

In his book *The Call to Discipleship*, Karl Barth writes about our tendency to adopt Christianity like we join a fraternal organization—it's a nice thing to do, and it fits in beautifully with our life plans. Sadly, we can tend to treat our call to faith with an indifference borne out of our jaded human experience where we've seen it all, done it all, and this is just one more thing to do to guarantee a healthy, happy life.

But the call to discipleship is a call to leave all behind and follow Christ. It means letting go of all that has gone before in such a way we hold loosely to the things of this world and we hold tightly to Jesus Christ, our new humanity. God calls us to let go of all of the things in our life we identify ourselves by, for our new identity is in Jesus Christ alone.

This can be very difficult, especially when what we need to leave behind is something we have built our whole life around, thinking it defines us and our humanity. Just what exactly are we willing to do for love? Just what are we willing to leave behind to follow Christ?

Perhaps if we were willing to look at this question from the other way around, we might find some compelling reason to leave everything behind.

We need to look intently at Jesus Christ—who is he? Here is one who lived eternally in a relationship of love and companionship in which he was content, fulfilled, and complete. He had no need of anyone or anything else. He did not need us, nor did God have any reason to create us other than as an expression of his overflowing, abundant love.

Yet this God, who was rich in every way, set all the privileges and dignity of his divinity aside and joined us in our humanity. He left everything familiar and comfortable and took up residence in a human body. He allowed himself to be carried about and mothered by Mary and to be instructed in the temple by the rabbis. He walked about on earth, getting his feet dusty and dirty like every other human being. And he did it all for love.

And this wasn't enough for him. He even allowed himself to be insulted, abused, shamed, and crucified by us. He died an ignoble death with a word of forgiveness and compassion on his lips. Isn't that the truest expression of love?

Taking all this into account then, how can there be anything we are not willing to give up for him? Love and gratitude for this amazing act of love compel us to drop everything and to do whatever it takes to follow him, even if it means leaving everything we value behind.

It will not always be easy to follow Christ. We will be faced with the decision at some point in our lives—do I cling to what is comfortable and convenient, or do I hold fast to Christ? Is this relationship I'm in more important to me than living in agreement with the one who gave it all up for me? Do I hold fast to my integrity or to the job I desperately need so I can keep my house? Will I hold on to my pride or be willing to eat humble pie and admit to my spouse I am wrong?

What are we willing to give up for love? Jesus gave it all up for you and for me—perhaps what we need to give up really isn't that significant after all.

Prayer

Lord, thank you for leaving everything behind and joining us in our humanity. Thank you for loving us so much you were willing to give it all up for love. Grant us the grace to give ourselves fully to you and to others in the same way you have given yourself to us. In your name, Jesus, we pray. Amen.

20

It's Tempting, But …
1 Corinthians 10:13

Temptation is real. Temptation is something every human faces, especially when it comes to our relationship with God and our relationships with one another. Falling prey to temptation is part of our human condition; none of us are exempt from the lure of sin.

As we look toward the gift of the death and resurrection of God's Son on our behalf, we can find comfort in the life Jesus lived and the death he died, because he faced every temptation we face, but he did not sin. We participate in his perfected humanity by the Holy Spirit, and in this way, we are able to endure temptation and resist the pull to sin.

It is normal for us as human beings to come up against something in our lives that tells us quite convincingly God is not to be trusted—that he is not the loving, compassionate God he is in reality. Life circumstances, the way significant people in our lives treat us, and our response to these experiences all play a role in the way we view God and whether or not we believe he is trustworthy and loving.

What we believe about God and who he is, and about ourselves and who we are, directly impacts the way we respond to the events in our lives as well as the way we respond to the desires and pulls of our broken humanity. The emptiness we may feel at times and the hidden dark areas we push down inside ourselves because they are too painful to face often drive us in ways we don't recognize or expect. Sometimes it seems that our behavior is beyond our control.

We may find ourselves addicted to substances or habits we'd rather not be held to, and we may find ourselves in relationships or circumstances that are unhealthy and destructive, but we don't know how to step away from them and move on. We may hear some preacher say we need to repent and put sin out of our lives, but sin doesn't hear the sermon and stays in spite of all our efforts to get rid of it.

If facing temptation is a common human experience, and temptation is something Jesus faced alongside each one of us during his life here on earth, then we need to understand being tempted to do or say or be something that does not express love for God or others is not a sin in itself. Temptation happens. How we face that temptation will determine whether we will endure and resist it, or whether we will give in to it.

The key, when it comes to resisting temptation, has to do with our relationship with God in Christ through the Spirit. We need first to understand God is faithful. He would not allow us to be tempted if he hadn't first provided us with what we needed to overcome that temptation and to resist it. And he did this—he gave us Jesus Christ and the Spirit.

Jesus Christ endured the same temptations and yet did not sin, no matter how enticing those temptations were. His perfected humanity is ours through the gift of the Holy Spirit. Through the Spirit, Jesus dwells in our hearts. The "mystery of godliness" the apostle Paul said, is "Christ in you, the hope of glory." Christ in us by the Spirit is what we need to overcome every temptation and resist it. Christ did it, and we participate in that finished work by the Spirit in us.

When we are living in intimate relationship with the Father, through Jesus Christ and in the Holy Spirit, in a daily walk with God that involves transparency, authenticity, humility, and an acknowledgment of our dependency upon God for all things, temptations begin to be seen for what they are. We begin to see temptations as invitations to break fellowship with God and others.

When we experience the broken relationships, alienation, and separation that come with yielding to temptation, and we face the pain that comes with the consequences of our sins, this can be a springboard to a deeper relationship with God. It is God's mercy and kindness that bring us to the place of repentance so we will give up our idolatries, our immorality, and our ingratitude toward God.

When we have experienced what it is like to walk in a close relationship with God, where the Spirit begins to work to transform us, and we encounter Christ in a personal, intimate communion, we find that we don't want to do anything that will mar or break that relationship. We won't want to offend or insult or harm God or others in any way. This is Christ in us—God's heart and mind are beginning to become ours. This is our best resistance to temptation.

Granted, we do participate in the process of resisting temptation. We do this by growing in and deepening our relationship with God. We open ourselves up to the Holy Spirit and invite him to grow Christ in us, and we do this by practicing spiritual disciplines such as prayer, meditation on God and his Word, meeting together for worship and fellowship, reading the Word of God, caring for others, and participating in small groups.

We may need to practice a spiritual discipline that offers up to God our commitment to put away things that cause us to be tempted to do what is wrong. We may need to eliminate certain things or particular relationships out of our daily existence because they cause us to be tempted to break fellowship with God or others. We may need to stop listening to or watching things that encourage us to participate in ungodly ways of living or being.

Not all of us are strong in every area of our lives to where we are never tempted in some way. It is foolish to constantly tempt ourselves, especially when God is calling us to put off the old self that is dead and to put on our new self, which was given to us in Christ Jesus. Part of our participation in Christ's perfected humanity involves choosing to live in agreement with the King of the kingdom of God rather than insisting on being a law unto ourselves.

But ultimately, we will face temptations that seem beyond our ability to resist. We will have areas in our lives where we cannot seem to overcome some flaw, fault, or sin. We will struggle in some areas, and no matter how hard we try to resist the temptation, we fail. God will, more than once, bring us to the place where we have to recognize and acknowledge we are incapable of resisting sin on our own. We are incapable of perfection in this life—it cannot be done by us on our own.

God says to you and to me—accept the reality of your need for grace. Turn to Christ. He is your perfected humanity; he is your life. Respond to the gift of the Spirit God has given you. Open yourself to the work he is trying to do in you and in your life even now. God is at work in you, providing the way of escape from temptation and enabling you to endure the temptations you are facing. He is faithful. He will not stop until he has finished what he began in you—to reveal Christ in you. Praise his holy name.

Prayer

Lord Jesus, I thank you that you endured every temptation you faced and you did not sin. And thank you for sharing this perfect resistance against temptation with us by the Spirit. I pray, Father, you will finish the work you have begun in us so we might fully reflect the image of Christ and so, by your Spirit, we may live in close fellowship with you and one another. We look forward to an eternity spent in gracious, loving communion with you and one another. In your name, we pray. Amen.

21

"Is it Love or Is It Magic?"
John 13:34–35

A while back, I was watching an old classic TV series about a nanny who helps a professor care for his three children. She has a knack for knowing exactly what is needed in every situation. She always seems to know who's at the door before they knock or who's on the phone before it rings. At the beginning of each show, we hear the question being asked about all the amazing things she does, whether it is love or if it is magic. And it is left up to the audience to decide.

I think sometimes the current interest in all types of spirituality blurs the lines for us between what is magic and what is love. Whether we like it or not, our view of God and spirituality is influenced by our culture and all we see and hear in the media. What we believe about love and being loving is also affected.

The apostle John wrote: "God is love." That, I believe, is a true statement. But what does it mean?

Does "God is love" mean that love is God? No. Love is a relational property, something expressed. Love in itself is not a being. God is a being, who is Father, Son, and Spirit, who lives in love—love describes his being. It describes how he lives in mutual submission, caring, and oneness—in perichoresis.

So, if God is love, does this mean God has to always do nice things for us? I mean, if God is love, how come there are so many nasty things going on in the world—so many hurt people, ruined lives—so much rampant evil? How can God be love and let that happen?

Well, no, God isn't a magical nanny who's going to make everything wonderful for us all the time. And he's not obligated to do this, even if he is love. Love doesn't equate automatically with being nice all the time.

And love doesn't equate with God giving us what we want all the time. There is no magic formula for getting what we want from God. If there were, this would mean we worship a magical God that we can control and use. Magic is something we use to try to manipulate spiritual realities, but God is a being who refuses to be used or manipulated by us.

God just doesn't work that way. God is completely free to do whatever he wants, whenever he wants, however he wants. He's totally free, but he's also totally love. And he loves us enough that he does not allow us to control, manipulate, or use him. He does, rather, allow us to influence him as a child may influence a parent to say yes to his request for a new puppy.

God teaches us through Jesus that real love is serving, sacrificial, and never works in opposition to what is right, pure, holy, and true. Real love is relational in a heavenly way. Real love calls out the best in people—raising them up to be all God intended them to be when he created them in the first place—a true reflection of himself. Sometimes this means saying, "No!" or putting boundaries in a relationship. Sometimes real love hurts, causing or experiencing suffering in order to help and heal. Sometimes love allows people to feel the full impact of the consequence of their choices—not to hurt them but to motivate them to repent and change. God does this with us.

Much of the evil and suffering we see and experience is the result of our own choices and our own stubborn willfulness. We inflict it on one another, even sometimes without realizing we are doing it. We don't always make decisions out of a heart of love, so suffering, pain, and death result.

I believe there is a huge difference between magic and love, one God demonstrates to us through his Son, Jesus Christ. Real love can be seen and experienced in a personal relationship with God in Christ by the Spirit. Real love can be seen and experienced as we reflect God in Christ by the Spirit in our relationships with one another.

But God isn't interested in our magic incantations, our self-help programs, or worship rituals we use to try to somehow get God to do what we want—to try to fix problems or heal people. God can do that all by himself and often does do that without any of our help. He likes to include us in his miracles—but only as participants, not as magicians. It's not about magic; it's all about love.

Prayer

Holy God, forgive us, please, for all the times and ways in which we try to manipulate, control, and use you. Forgive us for seeing you as something to fix things with rather than as a person to relate to in love. Thank you. Your great love goes beyond anything we can ask or imagine, and you have our best interests at heart all the time. Perfect us in your holy love in Jesus. In your name—Father, Son, and Spirit—you who alone are God. Amen.

22

Is Grace Really Enough?
2 Corinthians 12:7–9

Have you ever wondered why God doesn't fix things? Why doesn't he fix this broken world? If God is such a great, awesome being, why doesn't he fix everything when we ask him to?

Specifically, why does God allow us to keep stumbling over and over again in the same way when we continually are asking him to help us change and be different? Are people who are chronic sinners covered by grace, or are they somehow outside the limits of grace, in some place of condemnation, headed straight for Gehenna?

Do you ever think about questions like this? These are the tough questions of life. And there are no easy answers. It is questions like these that caused Martin Luther to question Catholicism and to tack his objections on a church door. And he had good reasons for his objections. When is grace not enough? Is there a limit to grace? Is grace an umbrella under which only a few can stand, and the rest (those "heathens") are left outside?

Salvation is, as Paul wrote, not something earned, but "by grace you have been saved through faith; and that not of yourselves, it is the gift of God" (Eph. 2:8 NASB). Every good and perfect gift, including grace, comes down from God, and he does not change his mind.

He cannot change his mind about grace because he has committed himself unreservedly and completely to humanity in Jesus Christ. He has united his Godhead with our humanity in the person of Jesus Christ.

There is no limit to grace. God didn't just commit part of himself to us—he committed all of himself to us by uniting himself with us in our human flesh in hypostatic union. There is no limit to God's grace because God didn't take up just part of humanity in Jesus Christ but all of humanity. As the church fathers said, what is not assumed is not healed. God's grace is unlimited.

But what about us? Is it all up to us to receive God's grace? What if we reject it? What if we turn away from it? What if we, even knowing the consequences, continually turn away from God's grace or abuse it? And what if we mess up after we have put our faith in Christ? What if our best efforts at "being good" fail?

Well, this is a topic worth wrestling with. If indeed all of humanity was taken up in Jesus in his life, death, and resurrection, then he stood in our place when he obeyed John the Baptist's call to repent and be baptized. He certainly didn't do it on his own account—he never sinned because he was God in human flesh. He did it in our place, making the choices we should have made and should make day by day and don't. Jesus lived the life we ought to live in relationship with God and others. He, through his life, suffering, death, and resurrection, was humanity's perfect response to the Father in our place and in our stead.

Whether or not we receive and embrace the grace offered by God is bound up in Christ's perfect response to the Father on our behalf. So, what is left for us to do? All God asks is we participate in Christ's life, death, and resurrection. This is why Christ is central to everything in our relationship with God and others. We participate in his "yes" to God in the face of our human "no."

The scripture says sinners will not be in the kingdom of God. For example, the apostle Paul writes that people who practice "immorality, impurity, sensuality, idolatry, sorcery, enmities, strife, jealousy, outbursts of anger, disputes, dissensions, factions, envying, drunkenness, carousing … will not inherit the kingdom of God." Since we as Christians have all been guilty of these things at some point, just like every other human being on earth, we all stand in the same place—in need of grace. This is why Jesus stands in our place even today as our high priest interceding on our behalf with the Father. This is why in Romans 8:1 we read that there is no condemnation to those who are *in Christ*.

When we realize this and embrace the gift Jesus has given us—himself in our place—we begin to experience an inner transformation. The Holy Spirit, God's gift to us of himself within us, begins to change the way we think, feel, and believe.

But it does not happen all at once. And indeed, there are things we will wrestle with throughout our life, whether physical, spiritual, mental, or emotional, which God will not immediately fix or remove. Whatever the apostle Paul's thorn in the flesh was, God didn't fix it. Instead he used it to keep Paul dependent upon his grace. It is in our humanness and weakness God's power works most effectively. We always and ever participate in Christ. Our mantra must be, "Not I but Christ."

When someone willfully sins over and over and turns away from God's grace—God's grace doesn't go away for them. It is still there. They can still participate by the Spirit in Jesus's perfect response to the Father. But if in the presence of that perfect love they live in rejection of it, they will be miserable. They will suffer all the consequences of rejecting the gift God has given them in having given them himself. Because they are denying their true humanity, they are denying and rejecting themselves. They reap the consequences of that inner split. Question is—when they stand in glory and face the one, Jesus Christ, who is both the judge and the judged—will they be found in him? And that is another question worth wrestling with.

Prayer

Lord, thank you for your perfect gift of grace. Thank you for the infinite measure of grace you have given us in Jesus Christ. Please grant to each of us repentance—a change of mind and heart—that will enable us to fully receive and be transformed by your gift to us of yourself. Thank you, Lord, for though we are imperfect, you have perfected us in Christ. Even though we are weak, in Christ we are strong. And even while we were yet sinners, you died for us. You are our only hope, Lord Jesus. We trust completely in you. Amen.

23

Growing in Knowing
John 17:25–26

I was sitting around the table at a restaurant a while back when a loved one reminded me it's important not to assume that I know everything there is to know about something but to be open to the possibility I might be wrong. Indeed, this is a difficult thing to accept for someone who grew up in a family where knowing the most about everything was held dear.

Over the years, I have learned that how much a person knows about someone is not nearly as meaningful and important as how well a person knows them in a face-to-face relationship. This applies equally to our conception of God and our Christian faith. I learned at an early age the value of learning everything about God and about the Bible. But it really did not do me much good; indeed, it proved to be damaging and restrictive—until I came to know God in a face-to-face, personal relationship.

A relationship with God is not just a button you can turn off or on. In a real way, it is a growing in knowing. Just like any other relationship, it ebbs and flows, has its ups and downs, and grows over time as we open ourselves up to knowing God more intimately and deeply.

What I know and believe about God has changed over the years, and it has impacted my relational knowing of God. In other words, my learning about God has gone through a maturing process, and because I have grown in the way I see, know, and understand God, it has transformed and deepened my personal relationship with him.

When we read the works of Christian authors, we may assume what they teach at the beginning of their Christian walk will be the same as what they write at the end of their life. But the truth is we are all on a journey with God throughout our lives. And what we may write at the beginning of our lives will not be the same as what we may write at the end, because we change, our character and circumstances change, our relationship with God changes, and our point of view changes. In every relationship of significance, how deeply one person knows another will change over time.

Because what we know about God impacts the possibility of our knowing God relationally, it is imperative we be open to the idea what we know about God may be wrong. Since each of us was created in the image of God, we were designed to reflect the nature of God to one another. The problem arises when the image of God reflected by significant people in our lives is something other than who God really is. In other words, we place the face of these significant people over the face of God. How well we know God relationally, unfortunately, has a lot to do with how well we relate to people who impact our lives as we mature.

Another factor that impacts the possibility of knowing God relationally is how we interpret and understand family, culture, church, and the written Word of God. Speaking for myself, I have experienced some major paradigm shifts in my understanding of all these things, but God has done this so I could really know and understand him as the loving, caring God he really is. God has slowly but surely removed these idols from my life so I could see and know him in his true nature. I still have a long way to go, and I know the mystery of who God is will keep me fascinated for all eternity. But I'm extremely grateful he is opening himself up to me more and more each day.

The story we find in the Holy Bible is God's story. When we read it through the lens of Jesus Christ, then we are reading the scripture through the correct lens. The Word in Jesus Christ came to reveal the true character and nature of God as Father, Son, and Spirit, a God who would lay it all down so his creatures would share life with him for all eternity. Even though we as humans have rejected this God who seeks a relationship with us individually and collectively, he still has done everything necessary and possible to ensure we are included in his divine relationship of love.

God never ceases to draw us to himself. He works throughout each of our lives and circumstances to bring us to a deeper understanding of who he really is and how much he loves us and wants to include us in his life and love. He allows us to reject him and live in a way that is in opposition to the truth of our being (made in the image of God), and we experience the pain and suffering that go with this choice. But he never stops pursuing us.

Because he is bound to us at the core of our being through his humanity, Christ is present in a real way in every moment and in every situation. By the Spirit, God is involved in every part of our lives. We are held in God's life and love—rest in this truth and embrace it. Awaken to the reality you are truly and thoroughly loved, and God seeks to know you and relate to you intimately. Let him be the one friend who will never leave or forsake you, because that is who he really is. Christ is your life.

Prayer

Father, thank you. In Christ and by your Spirit, you have included each of us in your life and love. Thank you for making us your very own. Awaken us to the truth: we are deeply and thoroughly loved. Free us from the impulse to run and hide. Remove the fear of being truly known and enable us to trust you to love us without condemnation or rejection. Enable us by your grace to live in the true reality of who we are in you. Through Jesus and by your Spirit. Amen.

24

Loving the Unseen and Invisible
Genesis 16:13

There may be times in our lives when we feel invisible. Everyone around us at work seems to receive the perks, and we get nothing. All our friends have a significant other, but we don't. Our life is falling apart, and no one seems to notice or care. Perhaps we come to a holiday like Valentine's Day and wonder why we, once again, have to spend it alone and forgotten.

There are lots of opportunities in life to celebrate pity parties. It seems to be the nature of being human to have days when life just doesn't seem to be worth living, when we feel forgotten and unnoticed by God and everyone else.

I am reminded of the story of Hagar. Hagar's story begins with her being forcibly employed as a servant to Sarah, the wife of Abraham. When Sarah could not have a child but Abraham had been promised to have an heir, Sarah decided to follow the customs of the time and have an heir through her maid, Hagar.

Humanly, it seemed to be a great idea, but the plan quickly began to fall apart. Jealousy, anger, conceit—all the human weaknesses seemed to be employed in destroying the family unit. Sarah beat her, and the frightened and pregnant Hagar fled into the wilderness.

As she wept in the desert for herself and her precious son, an angel provided her with water and told her to go back to Sarah. God saw her and her son; he saw the ones who were invisible. And God had an inheritance in mind for her son—he was not forgotten.

This encounter with God profoundly impacted Hagar. Hagar was one of the few people in the Bible who gave God a name—*the God who sees me*. She understood and appreciated the reality that God was not some ethereal concept or distant being in the sky. He wasn't just some manifestation of human consciousness. The God who had intervened in her life was real, powerful, and personal, and he cared about her. And he had come to her in the midst of her suffering and isolation.

So, what about you and me? It's not every day we see or experience manifestations of the divine. Life still falls apart around us while we do our best to hold it all together. Is there really a God who sees you and me? Or is this just another mythological story in a book? Is this just a nice fairy tale that was designed to make us feel better about ourselves and the world we live in?

I suppose a person could give all types of explanations about why you should believe in a real and personal God. I can share the testimony of scripture, of the God who created you and me, and loved us so much that he came to be one of us—to live with us, and die for us, and to rise from the grave. But it boils down to this—have you personally encountered the living God? Do you realize for yourself you are not invisible to him? Have you experienced the reality he sees you and loves you and wants a personal relationship with you?

Faith in the God who sees you in the midst of your invisibility begins with knowing he is real and he rewards those who diligently seek him (Heb. 11:6). God enjoys hide-and-seek, but he will not be found unless he chooses to be found. We seem to believe a real God will just show up and do what we want done in a situation. And when he doesn't do what we expect, we say he doesn't exist. But we aren't about to seek him out, much less let him tell us what to do when we do encounter him.

God gave us a really big clue as to how to find him when he came to us in the person of Jesus Christ. Jesus is the exact representation of God's being (Heb. 1:3). He is God in a tangible human being—the God who sees us lived here among us as one of us. Jesus died and rose again, and the testimony of the church is the Father sent through Jesus, the gift of the presence of God in the Holy Spirit to those who would receive him. So, you and I, as we seek God, have been offered the gift of God living in us by his Holy Spirit. The God who sees us now is the God who lives in us.

God sees you, and he sees me. He became you and became me in that he took on our humanity in Jesus. And God lives in you and in me by his Holy Spirit. As we welcome his presence within us, we will begin to experience the reality of the living God as being more than just an idea or mythology. As we hear the inner voice of the Spirit guiding us and teaching us, and as we experience the Word of God in the Bible coming alive and real to us and beginning to transform us, we realize the unseen God is indeed the God who sees us, his beloved and cherished unseen ones.

Life may still be hard, and we may still feel invisible, but when God abides in you and me, our lives are never the same. God may ask us to do the hard things, but we never do them alone. He is present in the midst of our invisibility—you and him, me and him, forever.

Prayer

Dear God, thank you for making yourself real to us in your Son, Jesus Christ, and by your Holy Spirit. Thank you, for we are not invisible to you but really and truly treasured, cherished, and understood. Make yourself real to us today—open our eyes to see you, and our ears to hear you, and our hearts to know you. Transform us by your grace. Holy God, may we bless and serve you forever, through Jesus's name. Amen.

25

Leaving behind the Ignorance of Prejudice
Matthew 6:33

One day I was watching with interest the speech given by Pope Francis to Congress. I was impressed by his finesse in taking the stories of four Americans and drawing from them positive principles by which our leaders and our people could move forward into the uncertain future.

As he was speaking, someone said to me, "Well, there's our enemy." It took me aback for a moment, but then I remembered how for centuries some Protestants have seen the pope and the Roman Catholic Church as being exactly that—as being the anti-Christ spoken about in the Bible. Of course, this requires a misinterpretation of scripture, but it has been assumed to be true by many and is still believed to be so by some today.

I'm a little ashamed to say I used to be one of those people who believed the pope and the Roman Catholic Church were the enemy of all that is truly Christian. This was born out of ignorance and false teaching I adopted as a child. But God was not content to leave me in my ignorance.

One of the first things he did was to place me in a relationship in high school where I grew to know and respect a teen who was the daughter of Polish immigrants. She had attended Catholic school in her youth and was a devout believer. She had a crucifix on the door to her room, and she would cross herself every time she passed it to go in and out. I saw a devotion to

Christ that was different from mine but equally, or perhaps even more, genuine. Although I had other friends in school who were Catholic, she left an impression on me that was not easily forgotten.

As time passed, I had a family member who married someone who was Catholic. I still remember the beautiful ceremony in her church. I could feel the presence and power of God there in a way that amazed me. The song that invited the believers to communion with Christ was inspiring and captured my heart. God was slowly and surely destroying the arrogance in me that kept me believing my faith was superior to and more real than these Catholic believers.

In the years since then, God placed me in the position of coming to know more and more people of the Catholic faith. Many of them were devout, and some were actively pursuing a relationship with Jesus Christ. Sure, there were an equal number who were merely nominal Christians, whose faith was just something they adopted as part of their family heritage. But what God did over the years was bring me to a repentance, a change in my mind and heart and in my beliefs, about the Roman Catholic Church and its followers.

The way God changed my mind and heart was by placing me in relationships with people where I was forced to reevaluate what I believed and why I believed it. I could have been stubborn and refused to acknowledge and repent of my prejudice. But my personal integrity would not allow me to do that. The truth was I was wrong, and I needed to admit it and change accordingly.

I have found, as time has gone by, that God keeps me in a continual state of needing to reevaluate, repent, and change when it comes to what I believe about certain people, their beliefs and cultures.

Technology is making our world smaller by bringing together people and cultures that would probably otherwise never interact. We are being forced to build relationships with people of all faiths and political and economic backgrounds. We are being forced to reevaluate what we believe about them and how we should interact with them.

This is actually a good thing. Because one day, in our eternal future, lies a time when all peoples of all nations and all cultures will be joined together in a world that has no political, religious, or cultural boundaries. In this place, what will matter most will not be what clothes we wear, how much money we make, or what kind of foods we prefer to eat. Rather, what will really matter will be our relationships with one another and with God. What will really count is how well we love and care for one another.

This is why Jesus said, "Seek first the kingdom of God and his righteousness ..." (Matt. 6:22 NASB). To have these heavenly values is more important than seeking the earthly values that are transitory and passing. We look beyond the human designations that separate us into the heavenly qualities that unite us. We are all one in Jesus Christ; he is our humanity—our unity, our equality, and our uniqueness. He joins us together in such a way that all these other things we count as important become truly insignificant in the long run.

Our challenge is to remain in an attitude of a willingness to see and admit to our prejudices and to consciously make an effort to change when we see we are wrong. When we respond to the work of the Holy Spirit as he brings us together with others we may feel uncomfortable with, we will find an amazing harmony and healing that can only be explained as divine.

God wants his children to be joined together with him in Christ, and when we respond to him, miracles happen in our relationships. We experience his divine life and love in a multitude of ways as we yield to the Spirit's work to bind us all together as one in Christ. May we always respond in faithful obedience to him.

Prayer

Thank you, God, for the amazing ways you bring healing and restoration in our broken relationships. Grant each of us the heart and mind to repent of our prejudices and to open ourselves to making room for others in the divine fellowship. We have so far to go! May we always turn to you for the love and grace we need so that we may love and forgive others. In Jesus's name and by your Spirit. Amen.

26

Intercellular Living
Romans 12:3–5

One of the most difficult ministry experiences I've had has been to be with members of my congregations as they go through the process of watching a loved one die of cancer. The strength they show in fighting this awful disease, dealing with the heartbreak and loss, and rebuilding after loss has been awesome and is a testimony to the grace and power of God. Losing a loved one is devastating, but it seems even more so when a family has had to watch the loved one suffer and die slowly and progressively, whether from cancer or some other long-term disease.

Cancer, specifically, is so destructive to the human body. The building blocks of the body—the cells—are a part of the body and are meant to help build up and sustain it. Cancer cells are cells that have turned into something they were never meant to be and have subsequently attacked the body.

I read somewhere cancer can occur when there is a loss of cell-to-cell interaction. When proper contact with neighboring cells is prevented from happening, cells become stunted and begin to collect into tumors, and the unhealthy cells spread into other organs and places in the body. As the cancer continues, it eventually spreads into the blood stream and lymph system and is carried throughout the body. And in time, and often after much suffering, the body dies.

Death, of course, happens to each of us at some point in our lives. It is inevitable. But I don't believe God ever intended any of us to have to go through the suffering and horror of cancer.

Yet it happens. It happens because we are frail and flawed human beings, and we live in a broken world. It happens because we attempt to step away from and live apart from the God who designed and made us and the world we live in.

Thankfully, this life is not the end—God never meant it to be. He always meant for us to live in eternity with him in glorified human bodies that are strong, beautiful, and whole and in relationships with him and one another that are healthy and intricately intertwined by love and grace through Christ in the Spirit—just like the intricately intertwined relations of the cells in a healthy human body.

Even though the apostle Paul probably did not know what a cell was, his description of human interaction in the body of Christ reflects the truth of how we have been intertwined together by the Holy Spirit into one body in Christ. When we lose healthy interaction with one another, we begin to destroy one another instead of building one another up. When we believe what is not true about God, about ourselves and others, and act on those beliefs, we begin to destroy not only ourselves but the body of Christ as a whole. This is also just as true in our communities, our state, nation, and the world.

Even though we often try to live like it isn't true, none of us exists apart from someone else. We were created to live in loving relationship with the Creator and one another. We were designed to exist in intricately woven webs of relationships that require healthy interaction and reciprocal caring in order to function in the best way possible.

We were each created uniquely, not so we would be separate from one another but so we would all fit together into a united, well-coordinated whole—a body. This body's life was given to us in Jesus Christ and has its source in the Holy Spirit.

Because there is one Spirit manifested in many ways, we are each unique and yet one. Just as a blood cell is not the same as a brain cell or a skin cell, none of us are the same. But the human body would not be what it should be if it did not have all three and every other different type of cell it needs to be whole and well.

When a person lives in a way that is contrary to their design by God, when they are abusive, selfish, fearful, or hurtful to others, then they are like a stunted cancer cell. Such a person influences, affects, and harms other people around them, who in turn harm, wound, and corrupt others—just as cancer cells metastasize and spread.

When society, culture, cities, nations, organizations, and churches become twisted and unhealthy, it is because the individuals within have lost their center in Jesus Christ. They are living out of their human brokenness instead of in the Spirit of life as God originally created them to live—in healthy relationship with God and one another. A cancer is created, which in time, if unchecked, destroys families, churches, communities, organizations, cities, and nations.

So, is cancer inevitable? Will cancer always win? Where's the hope in this?

Our only hope is what it always has been from the beginning—in the God who loves us so much that he came himself in the Word, took on our human flesh, and cleansed and healed it with his own divine presence. Jesus Christ is the answer because he is the whole, cleansed, and purified human we were all meant to be. He lived the life we were meant to live, suffered our pains, died our broken death, and rose from the grave. He took our human flesh into the presence of God and gave us the gift of his blessed presence in the Holy Spirit so, as we trust in Jesus, we may be regenerated or made new.

In Jesus Christ, every broken, cancerous cell in the human body, both individually and collectively, has been healed, cleansed, and restored. God has declared us in his Son to be whole and well. He is offering to you and to me life in Jesus Christ by the indwelling Holy Spirit. When we receive and embrace this, believing this truth and living accordingly, our hearts, minds, and lives begin to be healed and transformed. Our bodies may fail and die, but we will live on in the presence of God forever.

The corrupting cancers of sin, self, and Satan have been neutralized and transformed by the healing presence of the life-giving Spirit in Christ. Death has been defeated. Jesus triumphed over the cancers of evil, sickness, and death. They can only make a big noise, bluster, and try to cause pain, fear, and suffering and to destroy our faith. But they have no power over us any longer. One day they will be only a forgotten memory. In the presence of the living God, they are nothing but a moment in the eternity of his love.

As we embrace new life in Christ and live in the intimate fellowship with God and each other we were created for, the cancers of sin, self, and Satan will be supplanted by spiritual, mental, emotional, and social wholeness and health.

Sometimes it is a battle. Just as we battle cancer of the human body with every possible instrument we have available to us, we battle these cancers of the spirit with the divine weapons of the Holy Spirit—receiving God's gift of salvation, trusting in Christ's righteousness, and believing and living in the Spirit of truth and the Word of God. And we are diligent and faithful in prayer. We use divine methods of treatment, but we do this in Christ. He is our life. He is our breath. He is the one who lives the life we seek to live.

It is the presence of the living Word within, the Holy Spirit, who reminds us we are God's beloved children and who guides us and teaches us how to live in healthy relationship with God and others. As we listen to him and grow up in this divine life, we become a healthy part of the body of Christ, of our family, our community, our state, nation, and world. Our true value and worth can begin to be seen and contributed to the whole. And this is what God created us to be in our own uniqueness and giftedness. This is the intercellular life God designed us to have from, with, and in him forever. This is worth living and dying for.

Prayer

God Almighty, maker of heaven and earth and all that is in them, thank you. Thank you for life and breath, for all you give us each and every day. Holy, eternal Father, we believe in and embrace the gift of new life you have made possible for us in the life, death, and resurrection of your precious Son, Jesus Christ. Thank you for giving us new life even now in Christ by your Holy Spirit—your presence within. Dear Jesus, we acknowledge you as our Lord as you are our Savior; we commit ourselves to live not in ourselves, our sin and brokenness, our guilt and shame, but in the forgiveness, healing, and wholeness we have been given in you. Be our life, be our breath, our healing, health, and wholeness. God Almighty, in your one name as Father, Son, and Holy Spirit, we pray. Amen.

27

Heart-Sharing
Judges 16:17–19; Isaiah 39:3–4

When I was a little girl, I was intrigued by the story of Samson. Here was a man whose birth was announced by an angel to his barren parents. He was set apart for God from birth, which back then meant he could not drink any juice or wine made from grapes, nor could he cut his hair. As long as he was separated for God in this way, God gave him supernatural strength by which he helped his nation overcome their oppressors, the Philistines.

This was all well and good, and Samson began destroying the enemies of Israel. But he had a small problem. His heart was not fully devoted to God. Many times, he gave his heart away to a woman and inevitably ended up in trouble because of it.

In the final scenes of Samson's life, we see the infamous Delilah show up. Delilah stole Samson's heart, and one night he told her everything in his heart. In other words, he told Delilah the secret to his strength. The heart that God had said was to be his and his alone, Samson gave to another.

This would not have been a problem, only Delilah was not a safe person for Samson to be sharing his heart with. Delilah took that knowledge, sold it to the Philistine leaders, and cut off Samson's hair. He became a prisoner of the enemy. They blinded and shackled him. He could no longer do the work God created him for.

Too often in life, we are not careful about to whom or what we give our hearts. Then the people or things we've opened our hearts to begin to wound us, destroying the beauty God meant for us to have and our usefulness for his work in this world. We find ourselves trapped in a place God never meant for us to be, bound and shackled. What begins as a moment of pleasure or a relationship of passion ends up as bondage, suffering, and maybe even destruction.

The story of King Hezekiah also tells us about the hazards of opening the heart of one nation to another. In this story, the king had recovered from a fatal illness because of God's mercy. Some Babylonian envoys came by for a visit to share the joy. Now, at that time, Babylon wasn't much of a country. Hezekiah didn't really think he needed to restrict what they saw, so he showed them everything. He opened the heart of the country completely to them.

There was a small problem with this. What Hezekiah did not realize was Babylon was on the way up. They were to become the next superpower of the ancient world. And Israel would be one of the nations they would squash. Opening the heart of his nation to Babylonian envoys was not a smart move.

The truth is there is only one person who can be fully trusted with your heart and mine. And he is God.

You belong in this universe he created. You were meant to have a place in God's story. He created your heart for himself, and he will do and has done everything he possibly can to protect and care for your heart when you give it to him. He honors your boundaries and will not push himself on you.

If you are willing to receive the gift, he has given you his heart in Christ in place of yours. He has given you a whole heart in place of your shattered one. He has given you a strong heart in place of your weak one. Your physical heart may give out, and you may die. But his heart in you will live on into eternity.

Heart-sharing. God seeks your heart and mine—he has given his fully to you and to me. The cost of opening himself up fully to us was the suffering we inflicted on Jesus Christ in his life and death. But the payment is everlasting life for us in God's presence through his resurrection. We need to be careful to whom and what we give our heart in the world around us. But we can freely and fully give our hearts to the one who completely shared his heart with us. He stands with open hands, his heart fully yours. Will you share?

Prayer

Abba, thank you for your heart of love, which is fully ours in Jesus Christ. Grant us the grace, the courage, and the faith to share our hearts completely with you. Amen.

28

God up Close
Genesis 22:1–18; Hebrews 11:17–19

Do you ever wonder just what to believe?

Sometimes there are so many sides to a story I begin to think someone just might be making it all up. It's hard to narrow it down to what actually begins to resemble truth. It's really hard to get to the bottom of it all.

Whether or not I am able to come to some sort of conclusion is often dependent upon who is giving me the information. Is he or she trustworthy? Can I believe what they are saying? Are they reliable? Dependable? Can I trust that they are telling me the truth?

If I trust someone enough to believe what they are saying is the truth, I will act upon that knowledge. What happens next is very much dependent upon whether or not he or she was telling me the truth. And whether or not my relationship with this person continues to be meaningful and deep depends upon whether or not they were telling me the truth.

I think most people can agree that trust is at the heart of and essential to any meaningful relationship. Trust can be broken and lost. On the other hand, it can also be built over time as two people spend time together and come to know each other intimately through shared experiences.

In one science fiction series I was watching a while back, two warring nations that are working to establish a treaty intend to meet together. The spaceship that is escorting their diplomats to the meeting place receives a distress call from a ship of one of the two nations on board. Apparently, their ship has been attacked and nearly destroyed by the other nation's vessel.

This person who asks the captain for help has, over time, come to understand and respect the escorting ship's captain through several shared experiences in which each assisted the other in spite of their mistrust of one another. But now, with both the warring nations on the starship, the rancor between the opposing groups comes to a head, with the captain and his crew caught in the middle. The deep question that lies between every one of these people and a solution to the problem is, "Just who can I trust?"

Isn't this really what is fundamental to life and to any relationship? Trust. Who can I really count on when things get tough? Who can I believe? Who'll be there every time in every situation when I need them? Who's the one with reliable and dependable answers in every circumstance?

And just like in this story, it is often not immediately apparent just who is telling the truth. The one group believes the others attacked and destroyed their vessel, killing over seventy of their people. The others believe the first group has been attacking and destroying their vessels for years. What neither party is aware of at that particular moment is there is a third party imitating, attacking, and preying upon both nation's starships. Finding out this truth is essential to the establishment of trust, to the establishment of a basis for meaningful relationship between the two nations.

In other words, it is essential for the development of a healthy relationship and the fostering of goodwill between two parties that they begin to get up close and personal. There needs to be a transparency—a revealing to one another the deep secrets of the soul that they prefer to keep hidden. There needs to be an opening up, a vulnerability—which could very well open them up to attack or betrayal. And there needs to be a realization that sometimes it's not about one or the other, but often something else entirely that is causing mistrust in the relationship.

When we read the story of God "testing" Abraham, we find God is wanting to learn something about him he could not find out just by talking with him. God wanted to know whether or not Abraham trusted him completely, and whether or not he truly loved God, down to the core of his being. I don't believe God ever intended for Abraham to murder his son.

It is instructive to note that when God called to Abraham, he did not run and hide, make excuses, or try to rationalize away God's instruction to offer his son as a sacrifice. He said, "Here I am," and he went and did exactly what he was told to do. He trusted God, believing that in spite of what he saw and heard, in spite of the circumstances, God was going to keep his word and work out whatever needed to be done so Isaac and his descendants would inherit God's promises. Abraham believed Isaac was safe in the care of God because he trusted him.

When we know God well and over time have built a relationship of trust with him through shared circumstances and going through tough times together, we are happy to do whatever God's will may be for us at the moment. Although God doesn't ask people to sacrifice their children, he does often ask us to sacrifice things we think are important—popularity, prosperity, giving in to our passions and desires, favorite unhealthy habits, and improper ways of relating to others. Whether or not we do as God asks is dependent upon whether or not we trust him completely, fully, to the nth degree.

We grow in faith and in trust over time as we walk with God through the circumstances of our lives. As time goes by, we experience for ourselves the reality that God is faithful, compassionate, longsuffering, and truthful. We find that he is completely dependable.

And we learn to trust God as we look at his Son, Jesus Christ. We get to know God's story, the story of his Son and how he lived, died, and rose again, and how he now intercedes for us moment by moment in the presence of the Father in the Spirit. In Jesus Christ, we see God up close. We see God's nature, character, heart, and mind. We get to know God for who he really is—a trustworthy person who we can believe and count on.

So, when we are faced with that age-old question "Just who can I trust?" we have a place to start. In our relationship with God in Christ through the Spirit, we have a basis for trust. We have shared experiences that teach us God is trustworthy. We have God making himself fully vulnerable to the place where Jesus was willing to suffer and die at the hands of the ones to whom he came to love and make himself known. We have a trustworthy God. Will we trust him and place ourselves fully into his care, believing his word and doing whatever he asks in every situation? Will we believe?

Prayer

Trustworthy Father, today I trust you to keep your word to me, to be faithful and loving and compassionate in every situation, and to finish what you have begun in my life and in my heart and mind in Christ, your Son. May I always reflect your perichoretic faithfulness and trustworthiness in everything I say and do. In Jesus's name. Amen.

29

Face to Face
Exodus 33:11a, 14

One of the hazards of a long-distance relationship is the inability engage a person in face-to-face conversation. Communication tools and software make video chats possible now, and I love the way we are able to see someone while we talk with them without having to make a long trip in order to do so. A conversation via computer may not be the same as having a face-to-face conversation, but it is much better than simply having one on the phone.

Face-to-face conversations have the advantage of enabling us to see the body language and facial expressions of the person talking with us. We are able, if we are good at it, to sense the sincerity and intent behind what is being said. We can often determine a person's mood, their hostility or friendliness, just by how they respond as they talk.

To some limited extent, we can have meaningful and deep conversations over the phone. But in order to have an honest and open relationship, we really need to meet with someone face-to-face. We need to be able to meet with them in person. If we want to get to know someone in a deeper way than just an ordinary, casual conversation, we'll want to get them by themselves and spend time just talking, face-to-face.

I love the way God made the effort to engage Moses in these kinds of conversations. In Exodus, we read about the relationship God built with Moses over time and how the Lord spoke to Moses "face to face, just as a man speaks to his friend." As time passed, their relationship grew to where they conversed just like we do when we are talking with a close friend.

We may think to ourselves, *That's just Moses. God doesn't have those kinds of conversations with ordinary people like you or me. After all, he is God. He has much more important things to do than talk to all the people in the world individually.* We can kind of grasp the idea of everyone praying to God, but God replying and having a conversation with each person? Now that's a different story entirely.

And yet, this is what each of us was created for. When God walked and talked with Adam and Eve in the garden, it was a prelude to what he had in mind for each of us. He created you and me for relationship—with him and with one another. He did not intend for us to live independently of him or of one another. We are created for interdependence, for intimate relationship.

And when I say intimate relationship, I'm not talking about a sexual or romantic relationship. I'm talking about sharing the deep parts of our minds, hearts, and souls with another person—sharing life and being at a very deep level.

I believe the current obsession with sexual and romantic relationships of every kind has short-circuited our capacity for true, deep relationships—the kind we were created for with God and one another. Our ability to use social media for relationships is great, but we need to be careful not to let this keep us from building deep, meaningful relationships with the people in our lives through face-to-face interactions. It is very easy to keep people and God on the fringes of our lives and never really engage anyone at any kind of a deep level. This is not healthy.

Going deep with people and with God in this way means becoming vulnerable and facing up to the mess inside ourselves. We don't want to expose our deepest hurts and brokenness to others, much less to God. And yet this is the path to healing.

Opening up these wounds to others, to us, or to God means facing things we don't want to face. We may have to change or deal with things we don't want to have to deal with. We may have to do the dirty work of dealing with family dysfunctions or grieving our losses. Sadly, we often prefer taking painkillers and finding other ways to numb our pain rather than facing our issues. But we weren't created to ignore our pain or to try to hide it—we were created to engage it and, through sharing it with God and others in healthy ways, to find comfort and renewal.

Face-to-face sharing is an important part of the process of healing. Getting real with someone about what's going on at a deep level in our hearts and minds is essential to our mental, emotional, and spiritual health and our physical health as well. We need to drop our facades and our false selves and just be real with God and one another. And this is not easy to do, much less safe. Not everyone can be trusted with our secrets.

But God understands our need for face-to-face conversations at this deep level. This face-to-face sharing is so important to God he came himself to share in our humanity. He became one of us—the Word in human flesh. He experienced what it was like to be born of a woman, grow up as a child, be baptized, and live as an adult, and he shared every part of our human existence. God came and met with us face-to-face in an even more personal way than how he met with Moses centuries before.

God wanted to share every part of our existence and be included in it. This was so important to him he was willing to take on our humanity and share all we experience as human beings, including death and suffering. And he did much more than that.

He brought our human existence to a new level by raising Jesus Christ from the dead and by sending his Spirit to dwell in human hearts. God's Spirit in you and me means God dwells in humanity—he meets with us face-to-face within our own human hearts. Nothing can be more intimate than that!

In fact, we cannot escape him now—no matter how much we try. Eventually he will open our inner eyes to see we have Christ in us, the hope of glory. We have God in us—Immanuel. Better than any video call conversation, we can converse with God in our hearts and have a dialogue in which, by the Spirit, God knows us intimately, and we can know God's heart and mind as well. Our conversations with God can be just as deep and wonderful as those Moses had, because God calls you and me *friend* and speaks to us in our hearts.

You may say, "How can this be? God doesn't speak to me. And that's kind of creepy, you know—someone talking to me in my heart." Well, perhaps it's not that God hasn't been speaking but rather that perhaps we haven't been listening.

I was taught to be afraid of any inner voice who spoke in my heart, and so I never listened. I ignored it and pushed it away. But when I did finally talk with God and invite him to speak to me and to help me to hear and discern what was his voice (and not the other unhealthy voices), I discovered he was speaking words of love and grace to me all along. I found God really does want to walk and talk with us and share all of life with us. And this has been the experience of many others who have sought a deeper walk with Jesus.

God has brought each and every one of us through Jesus and by the Spirit to a place where we are able to have a deep, intimate, face-to-face relationship with him. By growing in our relationship with him, we will find ourselves growing in our ability and desire to have deep, meaningful relationships with one another. And we will be living out who we really are—human beings, created for loving relationship with God and one another.

Prayer

Father, thank you. Through your Son and by your Spirit, you have brought us into deep, intimate relationship with yourself. Thank you for making it possible for us to have close, intimate relationships with one another as well. Grant us the grace to set aside time and space to listen and talk with you and one another face-to-face, for this is what we were created for. Through Jesus and by your Spirit, we pray. Amen.

30

Covenant Relationships and Our God of Grace
Genesis 17:7

One of the most difficult aspects of living in covenant relationship with another human being is coming to grips with the need for unconditional love and grace. Since for most of our lives we work and live within the idea of making and keeping contracts, much of our culture is based upon this type of economic and social structure. For this reason, when we come to our relationship with God, as well as the covenant of marriage, it is easy to fall back upon this type of thinking and being.

One day I was listening to Dr. James Torrance ask the question, "Is our God the Triune God of grace or is he a contract God?" His purpose for asking this question was to help his listeners consider the difference between a covenant and a contract. Most of us clearly understand what a contract is. It is an agreement between two people that can be broken if one or the other does not perform the requirements of the contract completely.

A covenant looks entirely different from a contract. Torrance uses the example of a marriage covenant to describe the difference. If we think a marriage agreement is a contract (if you do this, then I will do that), then whenever one member of the relationship fails to meet the other's expectations, then the relationship is broken, and each person can walk away from the relationship at any time. There really isn't anything to bind two people together if marriage is treated like a contract. You and I both know that at some point in any relationship, someone is going to fail to meet the other person's expectations. It's a given because we're human.

But in a covenant, unconditional love and grace come first. Two people agree to love one another no matter what may happen in life, no matter what they each might do, while at the same time understanding that whatever they may do or say to one another will have consequences for the relationship. The binding of the two people together by unconditional love and grace keeps the relationship intact even when there is a failure at some point by one party to meet the conditions of the covenant. Love and grace triumph over justice in a covenant; there is a willingness to forebear, to work through difficulty together, and to patiently call the other party to account if necessary.

This is what God did with Israel and what he did, in fact, with all humanity. God determined he was going to draw human beings into relationship with himself. We as human beings have so often broken our part of this covenant, just as Israel broke their part of their covenant with God over and over.

But God has always been faithful to what he promised. He loved us prior to us loving him. He forgave us prior to us even knowing we needed to be forgiven. His love and grace are unconditional. This is true covenant.

This is where relationships get tough. Are we willing to forgive the unforgiveable? Are we willing to go the extra mile? Are we willing to keep loving someone who is all prickles and thorns?

You see, God loved Israel unconditionally. Over and over, he forgave his people all of their unfaithfulness to him. Were there consequences to Israel's breaking of the covenant relationship? Yes—they experienced slavery, oppression, and devastation. Even though God allowed them to experience the full consequences of their unfaithfulness to him, he, in time, laid down his life for his people, as well as for all humanity.

God's love and grace were and are prior to any law. Law describes what a healthy, happy relationship looks like and what the consequences are when people don't live in ways that coincide with a healthy, happy relationship. God's love and grace were present and available even when Israel failed to keep their side of the covenant and experienced the consequences of it.

God's love and grace are also present and available to each of us, in spite of our failures to live faithfully and lovingly in relationship with our God.

Yes, God often allows human beings to experience the pain and devastation that come with living in ways that break this relationship. And this is where we need to rethink how we handle our covenant relationships. It is easy to believe in a marriage, if one person loves the other no matter what, then they have to accept whatever behavior the other person does even if it is harmful or involves infidelity or substance abuse. But we need to rethink that.

We are called to love one another unconditionally within the marriage covenant. If a person within the relationship is an addict and is causing destruction to the relationship and to themselves, is it truly loving to allow them to continue in that destructive behavior? No. They need to experience the consequences of their behavior, but in such a way that the covenant relationship remains intact if at all possible. Love calls the broken person to healing and wholeness and provides a safe place for them to begin to get help. Love does not leave them in their brokenness and enable them to continue their self-destruction. This is when love has to be tough.

When a person is unfaithful in a relationship, there is so much pain involved. The gut-level response is to bail out of the relationship. But if indeed unconditional love and grace come first in the covenant, then there must be room, if both parties are willing, to forgive and to rebuild the relationship on a new foundation of grace. When Israel was unfaithful to God, we see the language of divorce in Hosea—yet God did not divorce Israel. Instead, he came in the person of Jesus, laid down his life, and died in her place. Wow! Most of us never get to that place of self-sacrifice and forgiveness in our relationships!

To truly love and forgive is to lay down one's life for the other so that they can be and become all they were created to be as image bearers of God. The Triune God of grace teaches us what covenant love looks like—and calls us to live in this relationship with him and with one another. Consequences have their place in covenant relationships. Pain and sin will happen. But unconditional love and grace trump it all.

Prayer

God of grace and love, thank you for your faithfulness and compassion. Grow in us the capacity to love and forgive as you do. Teach us what it means to live in covenant love as you do with us. Through Jesus and by your Spirit, we pray. Amen.

31

Breathing God's Air
Genesis 2:7; John 20:21–22

Have you ever thought about how amazing it is you breathe air and how doing so enables your body to function in such a way that you live? The air we breathe can be filled with a lot of things besides oxygen, and yet we still are able to metabolize what we need. We take another breath without thinking about it and go on living.

This is near and dear to my heart because I had someone close to me who, in spite of receiving oxygen in copious amounts, was unable to assimilate it like she should. It is quite upsetting to watch someone desperately trying to catch her breath and not being able to, even though she has plenty of oxygen available to her.

This morning, it put me in mind of how God must feel when he breathes his life and his Word into us, yet we seem to be unable to assimilate it. The Spirit proceeds from the Father and always has, yet we can go through life without ever responding to his presence in us and with us.

We may be frantically trying to catch our breath, so to speak, in the midst of the horrors of life, thinking we are left alone to manage it all ourselves. But the truth is that we are never alone.

Psalm 139 poetically describes the real presence of God being with us and in us in every situation and circumstance of life. In light and in darkness, God is present. No matter how far we run, or how high we fly, or how deep down we dive, we cannot and do not escape the Spirit. Our life is in him.

Not only did God in the Spirit breathe into us our very life, but he also sent the Word to bear our human flesh, to live, die, and rise again in our humanity. And this Word of God to us, Jesus Christ, said that he would not leave us orphans when he died but would come to us. And he did.

After the resurrection, Jesus came to show all of his followers he indeed now bore a glorified human form as part of his divinity. And after his ascension, he sent a special empowerment of the Holy Spirit so that each of his followers would share in his new life and participate in his mission of seeking out the lost and bringing them home. Through Jesus and by the Holy Spirit, God breathes new life into each of us.

But it seems that we can have a lot of clutter in our lives that prevents us from breathing in God's good air. In fact, we often choose to breathe bad air—we ingest a lot of unhealthy things that damage or injure our spiritual lungs. Our spiritual clarity begins to dissipate, and we suffer spiritual oxygen deprivation.

So pretty soon, even though we are hearing about how loving and gracious God is, all we can see or grasp is he is cold, distant, hard, and unloving. Even though we may be told that we are a beloved child of God, all we hear or get out of the conversation is God expects us to perform perfectly before he'll consider we're worth his time or love. Our mind becomes confused about what it means to live in union and communion with God through Christ and in his Spirit.

Truly, we all have those moments when we seem to be suffocating in the midst of a room full of spiritual gas fumes. It's important, then, to pause and remember who the source of good air is. It's not that he has stopped providing spiritual oxygen for us, but that we may need to step outside for a while and take some time alone with him to recover. Perhaps there is something we need to do differently, or maybe even quit doing, so we can catch a full breath of God's air.

The spiritual disciplines are a way we can open up our lungs to a big dose of healthy spiritual oxygen. I have found several resources over the years that can teach us how to make room for God to restore and renew us spiritually. Our spiritual formation group studies Adele Calhoun's *Spiritual Disciplines Handbook*, and another popular book often recommended is Richard Foster's *Celebration of Discipline*. *Invitation to a Journey* by M. Robert Mulholland Jr. also is a helpful introduction to learning to walk in the Spirit.

Taking time for spiritual renewal is an important part of the life of a disciple of Christ. Even Jesus, in his humanity, took time to be alone with his heavenly Father and to rest. He sought solitude and conversation with God when he needed renewal. After tending to the crowds, Jesus knew that he needed to tend to his disciples and to himself.

A lot of times, we mistake our need for spiritual renewal for physical hunger or a desire for physical contact. We try to fill our stomachs or other appetites, when really it is our spiritual lungs that need some divine oxygen.

Developing a way of living that includes God in an ongoing way and that recognizes when there is distance in our relationship with God will help us to recognize and attend to the needs of our souls. Walking in step with the Spirit, communing with God through Jesus, will invigorate us and restore us. This is our life in Christ.

So how about just pausing for a moment and taking a deep breath of God's good air. He's got plenty to give you, and even some to share with others.

Prayer

Creator God, Redeemer of all humanity, thank you for each breath of air you provide. Thank you for breathing your very life into us and for giving us new life through your Son, Jesus Christ, and by your Holy Spirit. Renew us in you. Fill our lungs with your divine air, with its heavenly oxygen, and enable us to absorb and grasp the depths and heights of your love for us. You are our life. In Jesus's name. Amen.

You Blew My Mind

Because you blew my mind
With your unfathomable love,
You felt my pain
And shared my tears,
The twisted paths
Of the tortured years.

How can I not pour out my love?
Your grace—it overwhelms me.

O loving Lord, it's not enough that you
Should fill the evening sky with stars;
But then you must
Fill my life
With all your healing grace.

It's not enough that you should fill my glass
With sparkling liquid wet;
But then you must
Pour over me
Your deepest inner peace.

Wretched though my life may be,
You feel my sorrow.
You share my pain.
Over every mountain, you carry me,
And now I'm here,
Stunned by the grace you've shown me,

Because you blew my mind
With your unfathomable love.
You felt my pain
And shared my tears,
The twisted paths
Of the tortured years.

How can I not pour out my love?
Your grace—it overwhelms me.

About the Author

Linda Rex earned her M.A. from Grace Communion Seminary, studying works by T. F. Torrance, C. Baxter Kruger, and others. Linda loves writing, drawing, and playing her piano, as well as spending time with her two adult children, and caring for the congregation she pastors for Grace Communion International in Nashville, Tennessee. She also writes a weekly Trinitarian devotional Our Life in the Trinity (http://lifeinthetrinity.blog).